"This wonderful, practical book is full of help  of the brain, and integrating thinking and feelin[illegible] s and activities for kids and their parents. It's fun, to [illegible] ul. A real gem."

—**Rick Hanson, PhD**, author of *Resilient*

"Debra Burdick has done it again! She has written a very informative, easy-to-digest book to help children, parents, and helping professionals use mindfulness strategies to navigate through common life issues facing children with attention deficit/ hyperactivity disorder (ADHD). Since children with ADHD have trouble paying attention, the focus on present-centered mindfulness skills is very intuitive and effective. Her easy-to-follow structure, using 'For You to Know,' a case example, and 'For You to Do' for each tip, makes each activity very clear and engaging. A great resource for parents and children alike!"

—**Judith Belmont, MS, LPC**, author of the *Tips and Tools for the Therapeutic Toolbox* series

"*Mindfulness for Kids with ADHD* goes beyond the title. In fact, the skills in this book can be used by those of any age, including young children and their parents, teachers, and helping professionals. The mindfulness activities are perfect for parents to do with their kids, and also for teachers to integrate into their classrooms. The information is easy to unpack, expand, and apply to meet the needs of different children in real-life situations. The timing of this book is perfect with all the challenges in our world today to help our kids adopt mindfulness and self-awareness as a way of life."

—**Nancy Hayes, MS**, educator, special education coordinator, and elementary school principal

"Debra Burdick has crafted the perfect resource for children with ADHD. This book is filled with fantastic, age-appropriate activities that can help children maximize the power of mindfulness to control their symptoms of ADHD. Parents may find themselves using the book themselves as the exercises are useful to us all. Outstanding in every respect!"

—**Ellen B. Braaten, PhD**, director of the MGH Learning and Emotional Assessment Program (LEAP), codirector of the The Clay Center for Young Healthy Minds, associate professor at Harvard Medical School, and coauthor of *Bright Kids Who Can't Keep Up* and *Straight Talk About Psychological Testing for Kids*

"I know lots of kids who moan and groan when they hear that it is time to practice mindfulness exercises. But these kids have yet to experience Debra Burdick's book for children with ADHD. Debra has a keen awareness of what it takes to help children with ADHD, combining a unique blend of helpful therapeutic techniques and good old fun. Thoughtful and well written, this book is sure to be a hit with ADHD kids, their parents, and teachers."

—**Lawrence E. Shapiro, PhD**, author of *How to Raise a Child with a High EQ* and *The Secret Language of Children*

Mindfulness for Kids with ADHD

Skills to Help Children Focus, Succeed in School & Make Friends

DEBRA BURDICK, LCSW

Instant Help Books
An Imprint of New Harbinger Publications, Inc.

Publisher's Note

This publication is designed to provide accurate and authoritative information in regard to the subject matter covered. It is sold with the understanding that the publisher is not engaged in rendering psychological, financial, legal, or other professional services. If expert assistance or counseling is needed, the services of a competent professional should be sought.

Distributed in Canada by Raincoast Books

Instant Help Books
New Harbinger Publications, Inc.
5674 Shattuck Avenue
Oakland, CA 94609
www.newharbinger.com

INSTANT HELP, the Clock Logo, and NEW HARBINGER are trademarks of New Harbinger Publications, Inc.

Cover design by Amy Shoup

Interior illustrations by Zanne de Janvier

Acquired by Wendy Millstine

Edited by James Lainsbury

Library of Congress Cataloging-in-Publication Data on file

Printed in the United States of America

21 20 19

10 9 8 7 6 5 4 3 2

Contents

Section 3
Mindfulness of Yourself

Section 4
Mindfulness of Healthy Choices

Section 5
Mindfulness at School

Foreword

Since this book is written for kids, I thought I would write this foreword for kids.

First of all, let me explain what a foreword is. It is not the opposite of a "backword," and it is not the word you shout when you hit a really bad golf shot. Nor is it just one word. Rather, it's a bunch of words that come at the beginning of a book—before the main part of the book, which makes it sort of like an introduction, but it isn't an introduction because it is shorter, and, well, it is a foreword, and after you've read this foreword you'll know what a foreword is. In fact, you'll be able to write a foreword yourself. When one of your friends, or one of your teachers, or your parents, or someone famous you know writes a book, you can say, "I'd be glad to write the foreword for you." This person will be impressed that you know what a foreword is and that you are willing and able to write one. You can add, "I'd even be willing to waive my fee." This will impress them even more.

Now, let me ask you a question. Do you know who Debra Burdick is? She is the person who wrote this book. Have you ever written a book? Some day you very well might, if you haven't done so already. But then again, you might not. You might sail around the world instead, or invent a way to become invisible. Debbie is sometimes called "The Brain Lady" because she knows A LOT about the brain—your brain, my brain, everyone's brain. I don't know if her friends call her Debbie or not. Her clients call her Miss Deb. I've seen her online speaking, and she seems really nice, really smart, and really helpful, so I'm pretty sure we can believe what she has to say.

This book is about mindfulness for kids who have ADHD. I know, B-O-R-I-N-G! But guess what? It's NOT! It's actually REALLY interesting! And really HELPFUL! I PROMISE!

Do you have ADHD? I do. I also have dyslexia, but that's another story.

In this book Debbie teaches us how to train our minds to focus more naturally, evenly, effortlessly, happily, and joyfully. She teaches us how to have fun learning instead of having to struggle. I promise.

Once she explains what mindfulness is—it's paying attention without distraction, if you can believe that—she then teaches you how to do it, if you can believe that.

She then explains how to fix ALL KINDS of problems that come up for us all the time—feeling embarrassed, feeling like you're a loser, calming down during a test, dealing with worry, what to do when you feel really angry, and a whole bunch more—and she explains how to fix them in ways that are really simple and easy to follow. Like, she knows how to explain in ways you can follow and use and even explain to other kids, if you want to.

What I am saying is that this is an awesome book, and Debbie is an awesome teacher. She is SO GOOD. You really will like this book. But you do need to take it seriously. You have to pretty much study it to get all that you can get out of it. But what I am saying is that once you get started you will actually WANT to study it, because, unlike memorizing a bunch of stupid stuff, the stuff in this book will make your life better, happier, more successful, and easier.

So, please, give it a shot. Take your time. Do the exercises. Share them with your parents. I promise you, you will be glad you did. Soon, without knowing what happened, you will be practicing the ancient art of mindfulness. You can impress other people by telling them you are an expert in one of the most proven practices humankind has ever developed, and it is making your body, mind, and spirit better every day.

Read on, practice, prosper, and enjoy!

—Edward Hallowell, MD

A Letter to Kids with ADHD

Hi there! How are you? I am so glad that you and this book found each other at just the right time.

As a child with ADHD, you have lots of things to learn every day in school and at home. You probably already know that having ADHD can make it harder to do as well as you would like. You may feel like you have to work twice as hard as everyone else. You may get frustrated, stressed-out, tired, or angry, and maybe you even feel like giving up sometimes.

Some kids with ADHD tell me that school is hard, or they hate getting yelled at for not paying attention, or they feel frustrated and discouraged when they lose their homework after they do it. Some say that they want to have friends and they feel really bad when they have no one to sit with during lunch.

This workbook will help you with some of these things. It helps you focus on the important things and practice skills to help you concentrate, organize, make friends, and feel better about yourself. It includes lots of fun activities, such as drawing, games, and using your imagination to teach your brain to concentrate and to help you feel better.

Section 1 helps you understand what mindfulness is and prompts you to think about what you like (and don't like) about having ADHD so you can get the help you need. Section 2 teaches you to do what you need to do at home. Section 3 shows you how to understand how you feel and to find ways to feel better. Section 4 guides you on ways to get enough sleep, eat food that helps your brain work better, and move your body. Section 5 gives you skills you can use to do better in school and get along better with others. On top of that, there is bonus material available at http://www.newharbinger.com/41078 that will teach you new skills to help you create success.

Look through the whole book first to get an idea of what's in it. Then start with section 1. You can work on the activities in the order that you feel will help you the most right now, but you will get the most benefit from the book if you work through the whole thing, completing each activity. Be prepared to spend some time doing this. Don't worry if it takes you a few months. Perhaps you can plan to complete at least one or two activities per week. You can set a reminder on your calendar app for when to do the activities each week. You can ask an adult to help you with the activities whenever you need it.

Some of the activities involve guided imagery and meditation scripts for going within and using the power of your mind and imagination to create success in life. You will find audio recordings of these at http://www.newharbinger.com/41078. As you do these activities, download the accompanying recordings to your phone, tablet, or computer so you can listen to them periodically throughout the day. (Be sure to ask an adult for help with this, if you need it!)

Whatever you do, don't give up. It takes time to learn new skills and lots of practice to get good at them. Be patient with yourself. Most of the mindfulness guided-imagery skills in this book are very short; they may seem hard or uncomfortable at first, but, much like learning to ride a bike, they will get easier with practice.

The more you focus on completing the activities, the more you can change your brain and your life for the better and truly thrive with ADHD.

Okay. Skim through the book. Then turn the page to section 1 and let's get going!

A Letter to Parents of Kids with ADHD

As the proud parent of an adult daughter with ADHD, I know how challenging—and, at the same time, amazing and rewarding—parenting a child with ADHD can be. ADHD often makes everything your child needs to do and learn more difficult for both of you. Take a deep breath. Relax. Everything is going to be alright!

Take time to learn everything you possibly can about ADHD and what you can do to help your child thrive. Every day ask yourself, *What does my child need from me right now?* Keep in mind that children always need unconditional love, understanding, encouragement, guidance, and support. On the one hand, kids with ADHD often feel frustrated, angry, irritable, anxious, and afraid; they may worry that they are a failure. On the other hand, their enthusiasm, energy, intelligence, creativity, sharp wit, and ability to think outside the box can help them truly thrive and succeed.

This workbook is designed to help your child become more mindful of how ADHD shows up in his or her life, and to learn specific mindfulness skills that will help your child succeed at the normal everyday tasks that must be completed at home, in school, in relationships, and to live a healthy life.

Although the workbook is written directly to kids, you can help your child use the book and offer encouragement to stay on track if he or she is having difficulty doing so. Review each activity with your child, offer support in completing the activities, ask how or when an activity will be done, and offer reminders to schedule the activities on the calendar. Perhaps you can give an incentive to help motivate your child to do each activity, such as spending time with you or a friend when one has been completed. Together, review the benefits of each activity and help your child reflect on how doing an activity has helped.

Encourage your child to complete section 1, and then do the rest of the activities in the order that best meets his or her specific needs. For example, if your child is discouraged because she's behind at school, do activity 15, "When You Feel Discouraged," and some of the activities in section 5, "Mindfulness at School." If he has trouble getting to bed on time, do activity 22, "Getting to Bed on Time." There are benefits from doing ALL the activities, but help your child first do the ones that are needed most. Number the activities in order of importance of what your child needs to help him or her stay on track and get the benefits more quickly.

There are recorded meditations and worksheets that accompany some of the activities, as well as bonus activities, that can be downloaded at http://www.newharbinger.com/41078. See the back of the book for details about obtaining this material, and help your child access, download, and use it.

Be a mindful parent. Practice some of the skills in the workbook yourself and then do them with your child. Take time to be present with your child. Listen. Show your child that you understand. Show your love. Enjoy each moment with your child.

A Letter to Professionals

Whether you are a mental health professional, an educator, a coach, or someone who helps kids with ADHD in any capacity, you can help them embrace their unique gifts and abilities while guiding them and teaching them skills that will help them thrive and succeed.

This workbook is written directly to kids with ADHD; it provides them with mindfulness skills to help them thrive in every area of life. As a helper, you are in a strategic position to help kids get the most benefit from this workbook.

Here's a step-by-step process for working through the activities in the workbook with kids.

1. Do section 1. These activities provide the basis for doing the rest of them, so be sure that kids do the activities in this part first.
2. After doing section 1, skim through the table of contents with the kids and have them place a checkmark beside the activities covering topics they need the most help with. Then ask them to number, in order of importance, those they checked off. If they all look equally important, then they can do them in the order the book suggests.
3. Do the rest of the activities either in order or according to how the kids numbered them in step 2.

Do the following for each activity:

- Read through the activity with the children. Discuss what they need to do, when and where they will do it, and how much time they need to allow for it.
- If they are not doing the activity with you, *encourage them to schedule on their calendar app a time to do it.*
- If they are doing it with you, *be sure to do the activity with them.*

- After they do each activity:
  - Discuss their answers to the questions asked in the activity.
  - Explore how they implemented the skill.
  - Explore what they learned about themselves from the activity.
  - Discuss what challenges they had while doing it and how they did or could handle them.
  - Help them reflect on how they felt doing the activity.
  - Ask them how the skill helped them or might help them in the future.
  - Discuss how and when they will continue to implement the skill they learned.
  - If they didn't do the activity, discuss why not and what they can do differently this week to get it done.
- Help them stay on track.
  - Plan which activities to do next.
  - Find a time to do each activity, and encourage them to put it in their calendar app with a reminder alert.
  - Discuss and handle their objections to doing the activities, such as not having time, forgetting, not seeing why it would help them, getting distracted, finding it too hard, feeling overwhelmed, and so forth.
  - Remind them of the benefits, and explore how they think their life might be better if a particular activity helped them.
  - Explore how they motivate themselves (usually to avoid pain or gain pleasure) and what they can do to motivate themselves to do the work to learn and practice the skills in this workbook.

There are also recorded meditations and worksheets that accompany some of the activities, as well as bonus activities, that can be downloaded at http://www.newharbinger.com/41078.

Section 1

Being Mindful About Your ADHD

ADHD can make all the things you need to learn and do every day a little—and sometimes a lot—harder for you. It can also be a gift in your life in many ways. This part of the book explains what mindfulness is and then shows you how to be mindful of what you like and don't like about having ADHD. It also includes an activity that will help you pay attention to the most important things.

Activity 1 What Is Mindfulness?

For You to Know

Kids with ADHD often have trouble paying attention. Mindfulness is all about paying attention. When you use mindfulness skills, you practice paying attention, which will help you be more successful in everything you do. You can be mindful any time, such as when you are doing schoolwork, hanging out with friends, managing chores, taking a test, playing sports, or just going for a walk outside.

Jacob, a bright nine-year-old, had a lot of trouble paying attention. He was easily distracted by sounds in his classroom, by his classmates, and even by his daydreams. He tried really hard to stay focused and was embarrassed and frustrated that his teacher was always telling him to pay attention because he was off task so often.

His teacher told him he needed to be more mindful. When he asked her what that meant, she explained that being mindful was paying attention to something in particular, such as math problems or a reading assignment. He noticed that he was able to stay focused a little longer when he reminded himself to think about what he needed to be mindful of while doing his schoolwork.

For You to Do

Mindfulness is paying attention to what you are doing, thinking, or feeling right now in this moment. You are being mindful when you pay attention to one thing at a time, such as the task you are doing, what you are thinking about, how you feel inside, or what you see, smell, touch, hear, or taste.

Practice the following mindfulness process.

1. Think of a task you usually do, such as schoolwork or a chore.

   Write the task here: ______________________________.

2. What do you need to pay attention to while doing this task?

   I need to pay attention to ______________________________.

3. Think about what you need to pay attention to while doing the task, and then pay attention to that.

4. As soon as you notice you are distracted and thinking about something else, remind yourself to be mindful, and bring your attention back to the task you are doing.

5. Write down what distracted you: ______________________________.

Practice steps 1 through 5 while you do three tasks this week.

More to Do

Draw a picture of yourself being distracted. Then draw a circle around the picture and a line through it to indicate "no distraction allowed."

Me Being Distracted

Draw a picture of yourself being mindful. Draw a star next to the picture. If you like, you can use the worksheet at http://www.newharbinger.com/41078 to draw your picture, so you can hang it somewhere you'll see it every day, to remind yourself to be mindful.

Me Being Mindful

Activity 2 Mindfulness Vocabulary Words

For You to Know

There are many words related to mindfulness. By understanding the words that are often used with mindfulness skills, you'll learn how to practice mindfulness more easily.

Isabella was just beginning to learn about mindfulness. She didn't always understand the words used with mindfulness skills, so her teacher gave her a vocabulary list that helped her learn the skills more quickly. She had fun drawing a picture of herself doing what each of the words on the list meant, and this also helped her learn them. She understood the words better when she practiced using them in a sentence.

For You to Do

Here are the definitions for some words that are often used with mindfulness skills. Study each word and its definition. Then draw a picture of yourself doing each one.

- *Inhale:* Breathing in through your nose (or mouth). Draw a picture of yourself smelling flowers or a favorite food, such as popcorn or oranges.

- *Exhale:* Breathing out through your mouth (or nose). Draw a picture of yourself blowing bubbles or holding a tissue in front of your mouth and blowing on it so that it dances in front of you.

- *Notice:* Observing, seeing, or detecting something. You can notice what you see, hear, touch, smell, taste, and think, and how your mind and body feel. Look around the room. Draw a picture of what you notice around you.

- *Awareness:* Noticing or realizing something. Draw a picture of yourself bringing your awareness to what color the ceiling is or to feeling hungry.
- *Pay attention:* Concentrating or focusing your mind on something or thinking about something. Draw a picture of yourself paying attention in class.
- *Intention:* Something that you plan to do. Draw a picture of yourself setting your intention to pay attention to your homework.
- *Go within:* Focusing your attention on what's going on inside your mind or body. Draw a picture of yourself going within.
- *Tune in:* Paying attention to something. Draw a picture of yourself tuning in to how cold or warm you feel.
- *Calm:* Feeling peaceful, quiet, still, silent, trouble free, relaxed. Draw a picture of yourself feeling calm.

Inhale **Exhale** **Notice**

Activity 2 Mindfulness Vocabulary Words

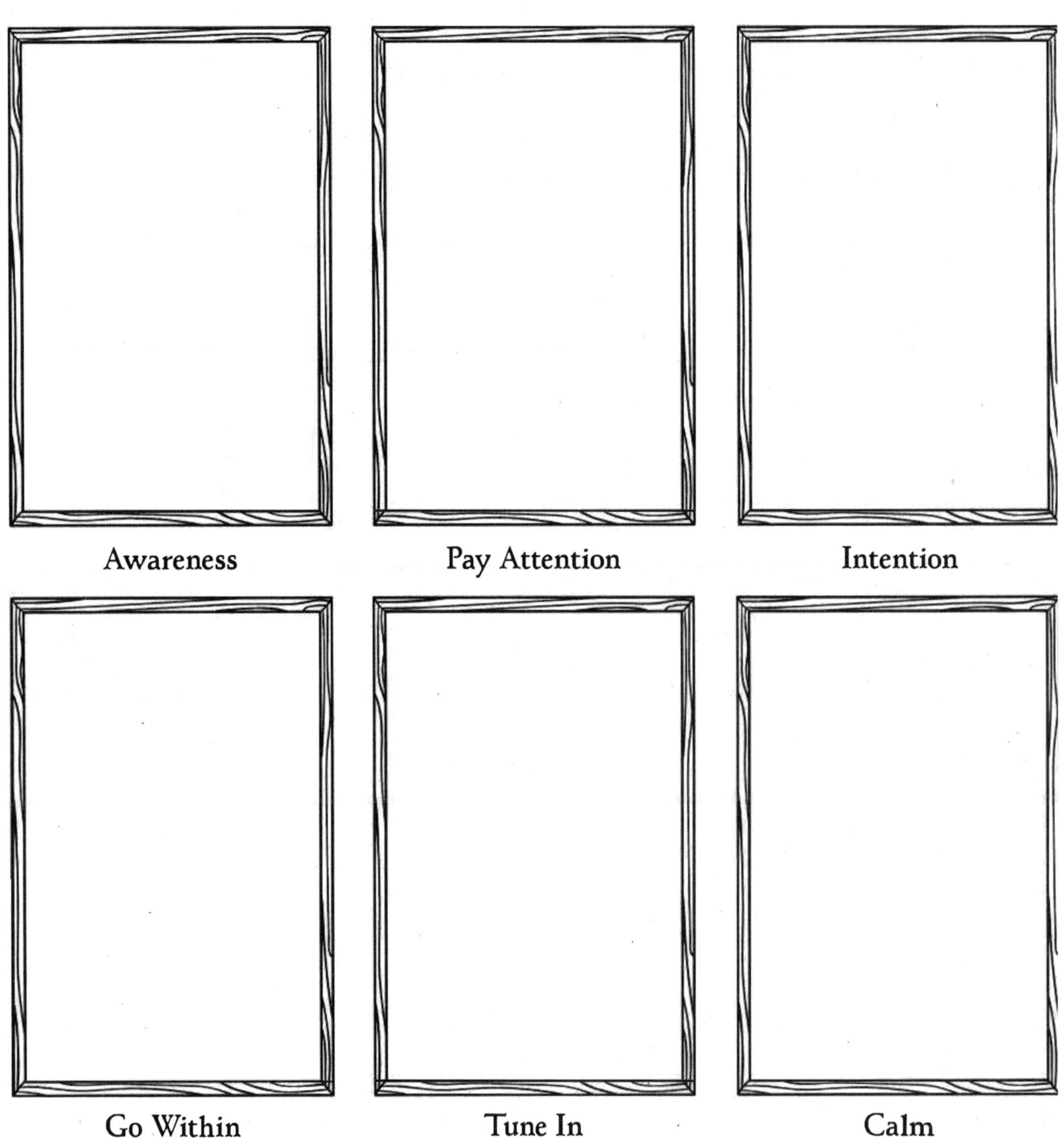

More to Do

Write three sentences using at least six of the words from the mindfulness vocabulary list.

Activity 3 What You Like and Don't Like About Having ADHD

For You to Know

Being mindful of how ADHD shows up in your life and what you do and don't like about having it will help you understand your ADHD. Then, to be successful, you can get help with things you don't like and focus on the things you do like.

Ethan often hated having ADHD. He made a list of some of the reasons why he wished he didn't have it. He often felt embarrassed when he got distracted and didn't finish his work on time. He was frustrated when he tried so hard to sit still and got yelled at for getting out of his seat. He wanted to have friends and felt confused and ashamed when his classmates teased him and no one sat with him at lunch. As he made his list he became more mindful of how ADHD made his life harder.

Then Ethan made a list of some things that he liked about having ADHD. He liked how quickly he could come up with new ideas for school projects or games. He loved having so much energy. He really enjoyed how easy it was for him to create something new, such as a design for a Lego project. He liked being smart and was often way ahead of everybody else with his answers in class...when he was paying attention. After he finished his list he realized that there were many good things about having ADHD.

What You Like and Don't Like About Having ADHD

For You to Do

Look at the list below and check off the things you don't like about having ADHD. Add more reasons you can think of at the end of the list.

- ☐ Am easily distracted or sidetracked
- ☐ Don't get my schoolwork or chores done on time
- ☐ Lose things I need such as books, pencils, coats, homework
- ☐ Don't concentrate long enough to finish tasks such as schoolwork or chores
- ☐ Forget to do what I'm supposed to
- ☐ Get yelled at a lot
- ☐ Lose track of time
- ☐ Don't keep my stuff organized
- ☐ Make careless mistakes
- ☐ Can't sit still long enough to get work done
- ☐ Miss what the teacher said because my mind is elsewhere
- ☐ Give up too soon or sometimes even before I start
- ☐ Annoy family and classmates with my hyperactive behavior
- ☐ Have trouble following directions
- ☐ Work twice as hard as my friends
- ☐ Say things without thinking
- ☐ Make poor choices—don't think about consequences

- ☐ Have trouble calming my brain down
- ☐ Get bored a lot
- ☐ Earn poor grades
- ☐ Have a hard time waiting for my turn
- ☐ Don't have enough friends
- ☐ Feel different than others
- ☐ Worry that I'm not good enough
- ☐ Don't know what's going on
- ☐ Other: ________________________________
- ☐ Other: ________________________________
- ☐ Other: ________________________________

Check off things you like about having ADHD. Add any more that you can think of at the end of the list.

- ☐ Creative
- ☐ Lots of ideas
- ☐ Lots of energy
- ☐ Eager to try new things
- ☐ Like a challenge
- ☐ Lots of interests

- ☐ Spontaneity
- ☐ Quick thinking
- ☐ Courage
- ☐ Lots of fun
- ☐ Good sense of humor
- ☐ Hard worker
- ☐ Great imagination
- ☐ Outgoing
- ☐ Playful
- ☐ Helpful
- ☐ Smart
- ☐ Adventurous
- ☐ Think big
- ☐ Think outside the box
- ☐ Hyperfocus
- ☐ Leadership abilities
- ☐ Other: ______________________________
- ☐ Other: ______________________________
- ☐ Other: ______________________________

More to Do

Draw a picture of yourself doing something that ADHD made harder.

ADHD Made This Harder

Draw a picture of yourself doing something that ADHD made easier.

ADHD Made This Easier

Visit http://www.newharbinger.com/41078 to explore the bonus activity "What Would You Like to Change About Yourself, Your Life, or Both?" and to download the audio recording of the "Mental Rehearsal" meditation to help you succeed.

Activity 4

What Do You Need Help With?

For You to Know

Everyone needs help sometimes, so don't be embarrassed to ask for it. You can list things you need help with. Then you can ask for the help you need, and it will be easier to do what you need to do.

Michael often fell behind in his schoolwork and didn't finish his homework on time. He also had trouble making friends and longed for someone to eat lunch with and to play his favorite video games with. All these issues left him feeling lonely and stressed-out.

With his therapist, Michael made a list of what he needed help with. Then his therapist helped him find people who could give him the help he needed.

For You to Do

Circle the things you need help with. If you are not sure what you need help with, ask an adult who knows you well, such as a parent, teacher, or therapist, for assistance.

- Paying attention
- Finishing schoolwork in class
- Keeping track of homework assignments
- Getting homework done and turned in on time
- Remembering what I need to do
- Following directions
- Taking tests
- Reading
- Math
- Making friends
- Talking too much
- Feeling stressed
- Keeping track of my stuff
- Organizing my books and papers
- Organizing my desk, locker, and backpack
- Sitting still
- Waiting
- Interrupting others
- Getting along with my brother(s) or sister(s)
- Getting to sleep at night
- Getting up in the morning
- Thinking before speaking
- Listening
- Other: ______________________
- Other: ______________________
- Other: ______________________

More to Do

Now that you have a list of things you need help with, you can ask an adult, such as a parent, teacher, counselor, therapist, or school social worker, to review your list with you and connect you with the people who can help you. Here is a list of people who might be able to help you or places where you might find it.

- Parents
- Teachers
- School social worker
- School psychologist
- Special education program
- Study skills class
- Social skills group
- Psychotherapist or counselor
- Tutor
- ADHD coach
- Other: ______________________________

Who can you ask to look at your list and connect you with the help you need?

___

Write about what you think will happen when you get help.

___

___

___

___

If someone helped you, write about how this person helped you.

___

___

___

___

Visit http://www.newharbinger.com/41078 to explore two bonus activities for creating success, "Setting Your Intention to Succeed" and "Using Your Imagination to Succeed," and to download an audio recording and script for the "Imagination for Success" meditation, which can also help you be more successful.

Activity 5

What Should You Pay Attention To?

For You to Know

ADHD often makes it hard to pay attention and stay focused on what needs to be done. The first step in paying attention is to know what you should pay attention to. You can pay attention better when you practice naming what you need to pay attention to.

Emma often had trouble paying attention. In order to improve her ability to pay attention, her therapist helped her practice being mindful of what the most important thing to pay attention to is in each situation that causes her to struggle.

First, she identified when she had the most trouble paying attention. Then she wrote down the most important thing to pay attention to in each situation. After doing this exercise, she got better at knowing what to pay attention to and, when her mind wandered, bringing her attention back to the most important thing.

For You to Do

Write down the most important thing to pay attention to for each activity. For example, for number 3 the most important thing to pay attention to might be doing math problems or answering the questions on a worksheet and finishing everything assigned. For number 10 it might be putting your toys in the toy box or your dirty clothes in the hamper.

1. Listening to the teacher: ______________________________

2. Doing schoolwork in class: ______________________________

3. Doing homework: ______

4. Reading: ______

5. Getting ready in the morning: ______

6. Getting ready for bed: ______

7. Doing chores: ______

8. Playing with a friend: ______

9. Talking to parents: ______

10. Putting my stuff where it belongs: ______

11. Riding on the bus: ______

12. Riding in the car: ______

13. Riding my bicycle: ______

14. Playing sports: ______

15. Participating in activities such as dance, yoga, art class, and music lessons:

______

16. Other: ______

17. Other: ______

More to Do

Circle the three activities above that are the hardest for you to pay attention while doing. Draw a picture of yourself paying attention to the most important thing during each of the three activities. For example, for number 1 you could draw a picture of yourself looking at the teacher while he or she is talking. For number 14 you might draw a picture of yourself watching the ball when you play soccer.

Number ____________:

I'm paying attention to ______________________________

____.

Number ____________:

I'm paying attention to ______________________________

____.

Number ____________:

I'm paying attention to ______________________________

____.

Section 2

Mindfulness at Home

Home is a good place to start being mindful. ADHD often makes it harder to finish chores, keep your room neat, and follow the rules. The activities in this part of the book will help you be mindful of how to do your part in your family, and how to follow the rules and get things done more easily.

Activity 6

Mindfulness of Doing Your Part in Your Family

For You to Know

Kids are often expected to do chores at home and help out with family life in other ways. ADHD may make it harder for you to finish chores, keep your room neat, and get homework done. Understanding your part in your family and being mindful of what your parents expect of you will help you get things done.

Ten-year-old Olivia has ADHD and felt like her parents yelled at her all the time when she was at home. One day they yelled at her because her room was messy, she forgot to feed the cat, and she played a game on her tablet instead of doing her homework. She hated how she felt when her parents were angry with her.

With her therapist's help, Olivia learned she that was an important part of her family and that her parents expected her to do certain chores and tasks. She learned that even though her ADHD made it more difficult for her to pay attention and finish things, she still needed to do her part.

With her mom's help she put a list of things she needed to do every day on the refrigerator to remind her to feed the cat, keep her room neat, and get her homework done. She set an alarm on her tablet that reminded her to look at the list. This helped Olivia do what was expected of her, and she noticed that over time her parents stopped yelling at her as much. She felt good about being able to do her part in her family.

For You to Do

Check off what your parents expect you to do. Ask them for input if you don't know what they expect of you.

- ☐ Keep my room clean
- ☐ Put my clothes in the hamper
- ☐ Set or clear the table, or both
- ☐ Help prepare food
- ☐ Load or empty the dishwasher, or both
- ☐ Get ready for bed on time
- ☐ Get ready for school on time
- ☐ Clean up after myself
- ☐ Feed the pets
- ☐ Get my homework done every night
- ☐ Show my parents and others respect
- ☐ Be nice to my brother(s) or sister(s)
- ☐ Get good grades
- ☐ Behave well

- ☐ Spend some time doing fun things with my family
- ☐ Tell my family about my day
- ☐ Do what I should do
- ☐ Do what I say I will do
- ☐ Tell the truth
- ☐ Follow the rules
- ☐ Listen when parents talk to me
- ☐ Ask for help if I need it
- ☐ Other: ____________________
- ☐ Other: ____________________
- ☐ Other: ____________________

Write about what would happen if you didn't do one of the things that your parents expected you to do. For example, the cat will be hungry and get sick if you don't feed it.

____

____

____

More to Do

List five ways you can do your part in your family.

1. ____
2. ____
3. ____
4. ____
5. ____

Draw a star next to all the things you did this week or that you will do next week. Write down how you felt after you did them.

____

____

Activity 7 Following the Rules

For You to Know

Kids need to know what the rules are and obey them. Sometimes kids with ADHD forget what they are expected to do or may do things without thinking first and thus break the rules. Being mindful of the rules will help you do what you should do, get along better at home, keep yourself safe, and feel better about yourself.

Alexander, an eleven-year-old boy, kept getting into trouble for not following the rules at home and at school. He often forgot to raise his hand before answering a question in class. Sometimes he got into arguments with a boy in gym class and forgot to keep his hands to himself. He talked back to his mother without stopping to think about if what he was going to say was helpful or hurtful. And he usually forgot to clean up after himself when he was done working with his construction sets.

Alexander's ADHD coach suggested that perhaps Alexander didn't really know what the rules were at home and at school. He helped Alexander make a list of the rules, which Alexander put where he could see them in his room and in his desk at school. Then he taught Alexander to stop and think about the rules before he did something. Alexander noticed that knowing exactly what the rules were meant he could follow them more easily. He loved not getting into trouble all the time.

For You to Do

Make a list of the rules in your home and place it where you can see it every day. Ask a parent for help with this, if you need it. Every home is different, but here are a few examples of rules: don't talk back, keep your hands to yourself, clean up after yourself, and don't jump on the furniture.

The Rules in My Home

1. ______________________________
2. ______________________________
3. ______________________________
4. ______________________________
5. ______________________________
6. ______________________________
7. ______________________________
8. ______________________________
9. ______________________________
10. ______________________________

Make a list of the rules at your school and put it where you can see it every day. Ask a teacher for help with this, if you need it. Every school and classroom has its own rules, but here are a few examples your school might have: raise your hand and wait to be called on before you answer or speak, follow directions, stay seated in your classroom, don't talk to classmates while the teacher is teaching or during a test, be kind to others, keep your hands to yourself, and tell the truth.

The Rules at School

1. ____________________
2. ____________________
3. ____________________
4. ____________________
5. ____________________
6. ____________________
7. ____________________
8. ____________________
9. ____________________
10. ____________________

Write about a time when you forgot to follow the rules.

____

____

____

____

More to Do

To make sure you are following the rules, use the Stop and Think practice before you say or do anything.

- Be mindful of what the rules are.
- Stop and think before you say or do anything.
- Ask yourself if what you are about to say or do obeys the rules.
- Ask yourself if what you are about to say or do will be helpful or hurtful.

Put this Stop and Think picture where you can see it every day to remind yourself to follow the rules. (You can download a printable version of this picture at http://www.newharbinger.com/41078.)

Activity 8

Remembering Things

For You to Know

Kids have lots of things to do every day. You may have chores, homework, sports, playdates, hobbies, and more. When you have ADHD it is easy to forget what you need to do. Being mindful can help you keep track of what you need to do and remind yourself when to do it.

Sophia had a hard time remembering what she was supposed to do. She felt frustrated when she forgot to do her homework and then got a poor grade. Her mother was often upset with her because she would forget to brush her teeth or would leave her backpack at a friend's house or would forget to bring her clothes to dance practice.

Once Sophia learned how to keep track of all the things she needed to do, she remembered things more often. She put sticky notes where she did some activities to remind herself what she had to do in those places. She listed her activities on a calendar and got in the habit of looking at it every day. And she learned the Quick Scan skill that helped her make sure she had everything she needed.

For You to Do

On the form below make a list of things you need to do and when and where you do them. Include homework, chores, sports, exercise, eating, playing, and anything else you do regularly. Ask an adult for help, if you need it.

Activity	*When*	*Where*
Example: Homework	Before dinner	Desk
Example: Girl or Boy Scouts	Tuesdays at 3:15	Youth Center

Ask an adult for help with the following tasks, if you need it. Place each activity you listed above on a calendar. Use different colors for things you do every day or week, for after-school plans, and for school projects. Be creative, and when you pack your backpack at night, look at the calendar to make sure you're remembering everything you need for the next day.

- Make a list of things you need to do every morning to get ready for school and put it where you can see it every morning.
- Make a list of things you have to do after school and put it where you can see it every day.
- Make a list of things you have to do before bed and put it where you can see it at night.
- Place brightly colored sticky notes where you can see them to remind yourself to do things. For example, on a sticky note write all the things you need to do in the bathroom in the morning and put it in the bathroom where you can see it; make a list of what you have to do when you get up in the morning and put it in your bedroom.

More to Do

Before you leave the bedroom or the house or the classroom, do the following Quick Scan to make sure you have everything you need.

- Stop and think about what you are about to do.
- Do a quick body scan while you say, "Do I have everything I need?"

  Notice what you are holding and wearing and make sure you have everything you need. For example, if you are leaving for school, make sure you have your backpack, lunch, jacket, or anything else you need to bring to school that day.

- Do a quick room scan while you say, "Did I forget something?"

  Look around the room to see if there is anything you are forgetting to take with you. For example, is your sports bag that you need for practice still sitting on the floor?

Activity 9 Keeping Your Room Neat

For You to Know

When your room is messy it is hard to find things, and this can be frustrating. Being mindful about where your things belong and putting them away will help you keep your room neat. When you make this a habit, you will be able to find things more quickly and feel less frustrated.

Ten-year-old Joshua didn't understand why his mother kept telling him to clean his room. He hated how upset she became with him because his room was always messy, but he didn't know where to start. Besides, he had other things to do that were way more fun than cleaning his room.

Joshua's ADHD coach helped him see how keeping his room neat was doing his part as a member of his family. He helped Joshua create a plan to get it clean and to keep it neat. Joshua found that as long as he was mindful about keeping his room clean and neat every day, it was pretty easy to do after all. Joshua felt better being able to find what he needed in his room and even better that his mother was pleased with him.

For You to Do

Look around your room, and if you see things that don't belong, take them out of your room. For example, throw away what needs to be thrown out, and put food and dishes in the kitchen.

Keeping Your Room Neat

List the items that belong in your room and where they belong. Ask a parent for help with this, if you need it. If you want, you can use the "Keeping Your Room Neat" worksheet at http://www.newharbinger.com/41078 so you can post this list in your room.

Item	*Where It Belongs*	*Item*	*Where It Belongs*

Label your drawers and shelves with the name of the item that goes there. For example, label the bottom drawer of your bureau "long-sleeved shirts" or a particular shelf "books" or "games."

More to Do

Set an intention to be mindful of keeping your bedroom neat and organized. Decide when is the best time to put things away every day, and put it on your calendar. For example, the ideal time might be before you go to bed, or after you finish your homework. If you have a calendar app, set an alarm to remind yourself to put things away each day.

Write the following statement on a sticky note and post it in your bedroom where you will see it every day. Fill in the blank with when you will put things away.

I will put my things away every day at _____:_____ a.m./p.m.!

Section 3

Mindfulness of Yourself

Kids with ADHD often get frustrated, angry, or worried when they try so hard to succeed and still get distracted, don't finish on time, lose things, or forget to do things. Being mindful of yourself can help you feel better about yourself and help you feel calmer, more content, and self-confident.

Activity 10 How Do You Feel Today?

For You to Know

ADHD can make you feel lots of strong feelings. Being mindful of your feelings can help you understand how you feel and then change to a feeling that feels better.

Ava had lots of feelings and often didn't like the way she felt. She worried that she would fall behind in school or get a bad grade. She felt bad when she didn't get invited to a party. Sometimes she felt like she was going to explode inside when other kids were mean to her. But sometimes she didn't know the names of the feelings she was having.

Ava's therapist explained that it is normal to have feelings. She showed Ava a Feelings Chart to help her name the feelings she was having. Then she asked Ava to draw pictures of herself having feelings that she liked, as well as ones she didn't like. She showed Ava how to help herself feel better by imagining she felt the way she liked to feel.

For You to Do

Look at the faces on the Feelings Chart and do the following:

- Circle how you feel right now with a red pencil or marker.
- Circle all the feelings you have felt this week with a blue pencil or marker.
- Circle how you want to feel with a green pencil or marker.
- Write about a time when you felt how you want to feel. Include where you were, what you were doing, and why you think you felt this way.

____

____

____

____

Feelings Chart

You can download a printable version of the "Feelings Chart" at http://www.newharbinger.com/41078.

More to Do

Draw a picture of when you were not feeling the way you like and what happened that made you feel that way. Use the Feelings Chart to name the feeling, and write the name of the feeling on the blank line below the picture.

I Don't Like to Feel ______________________________ .

Draw a picture of how you like to feel, and write the name of the feeling on the blank line below the picture. Then, make a copy of this picture, and post it where you can see it every day. Whenever you don't like the way you feel, imagine yourself feeling the way you feel in this picture.

I Like to Feel _______________________________ .

When You Feel Worried   Activity 11

For You to Know

Kids with ADHD sometimes worry that they won't get things done on time or that they will forget to do things. They may even worry that they aren't good enough or that they will never have friends or be a success. When you know what worries you, you can then use mindfulness to calm your worry.

Joshua worried a lot. When he took tests he worried that he would not finish in time, and sometimes he got a stomachache. He was anxious every time he went to lunch in the school cafeteria because he was afraid no one would sit with him. Sometimes when he even thought about going to school his heart raced, because he worried that his teacher would yell at him again for talking to his friends or for fidgeting in his seat during class. He always tried to do his best but often forgot to do his homework, and sometimes he lost it after having finished it.

Joshua's therapist told him that it sounded like he worried a lot. Then he explained that it is normal to worry sometimes, but it sounded like Joshua's worry was getting in the way of him doing things he needed to do. First, they listed the things that made Joshua worry. Then he said it sounded like Joshua was watching his worry channel a lot and taught him mindfulness skills to help him change the channel to one that calmed him down. After Joshua began practicing the skills, he noticed that he worried less often. And when he did worry, he could calm himself down and focus on what he needed to do.

For You to Do

Name three times you felt worried.

1. ______________________________

2. ______________________________

3. ______________________________

How did your body feel each time you worried?

1. ______________________________

2. ______________________________

3. ______________________________

Look in a mirror that's big enough for you to see yourself from your belly up to your head. (If you don't have a mirror, imagine you are looking in a mirror.) Point to where your body feels worry. For example, when you worry maybe your stomach hurts, or your neck gets stiff.

Now, name three times you felt calm.

1. ______________________________

2. ______________________________

3. ______________________________

How did your body feel when you were calm?

1. ____

2. ____

3. ____

Look in the mirror again and point to where your body feels calm.

Next time you feel worried, notice where you feel it in your body and then remember how your body feels when you feel calm.

More to Do

When you are worried, it's as if you are watching the worry channel in your mind. You can calm your worry by changing to a channel that feels better to watch. What two channels would you rather watch instead of your worry channel? (Examples include the calm, relaxed, hopeful, happy, focused, or fun channels.)

Channel 1: ____

Channel 2: ____

List two things you would put on each of your channels or draw a picture of them, or both. (For example, the calm channel might be a picture of pretty flowers, a calm lake, or you blowing bubbles. The happy channel might have your puppy on it, with you dancing or singing.)

Channel 1 ______________________________

1. ______________________________

2. ______________________________

I Would Put This on My ____________________ Channel.

Channel 2: ____________________

1. ____________________

2. ____________________

I Would Put This on My ____________________ Channel.

Spend a few minutes every day paying attention to what channel you are watching and noticing how you feel when you watch it. Remember, when you need to, you can easily change the channel to something that feels better to watch.

- Pretend to reach into your pocket and pull out your imaginary remote control.
- Change the channel to one of the channels you chose above, and imagine watching it for a few minutes.
- Notice how you feel when you watch the new, more helpful channel.

When You Feel Angry Activity 12

For You to Know

Sometimes kids with ADHD feel angry when things don't go their way, when they don't do things as well as they want to, or when other kids tease them. When you understand what makes you angry and how your body feels when you are angry, you can learn to let go of the anger.

Emily hated how angry she felt inside. Sometimes she felt angry when she was picked last for a team or when a classmate called her stupid because she wasn't paying attention when the teacher called on her. She felt really angry when she saw other students turning in their tests when she was not yet done with hers. Sometimes she couldn't control her anger and said things she shouldn't or threw things. One time she got so mad she tipped her desk over. Then she felt really embarrassed.

Emily's therapist showed her some skills to help her quickly calm her anger. First, he showed her how to blow her anger away by breathing in and then blowing out slowly, like she was blowing a huge bubble. Then he taught Emily to bring her attention to the bottoms of her feet. At first Emily forgot to use these skills, but then she remembered them the next time a classmate of hers turned his test in before her. Instead of tipping over her desk she took a deep breath, blew her anger away, and focused on her feet. She felt better knowing she could calm her anger before she did something embarrassing. Once she could calm her anger, she noticed that she wasn't getting as angry anymore.

For You to Do

Write about what was going on when you felt angry.

____

____

Draw a picture of yourself and add little *A*s where your body feels anger.

This Is Where My Body Feels Angry.

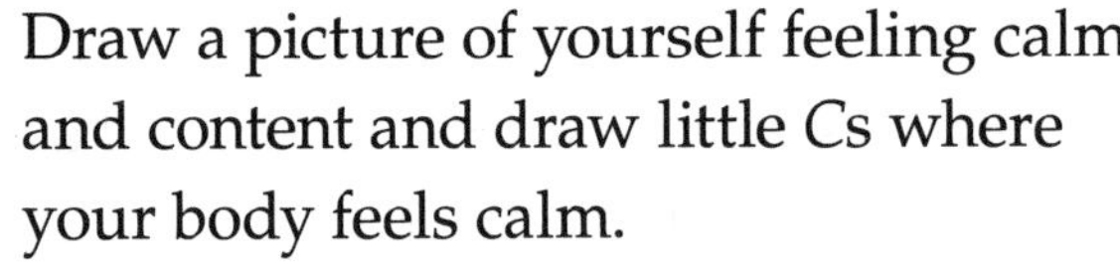

Draw a picture of yourself feeling calm and content and draw little *C*s where your body feels calm.

I Feel Calm and Content.

Any time you notice that your body is feeling angry, remind yourself how your body feels when it is calm. Then imagine your body is feeling calm to help calm your anger.

More to Do

Once you are able to notice when you are starting to feel angry, you can use the following skill to blow the anger away and calm yourself down while focusing on the bottoms of your feet. Practice the skill when you are not angry, and then use it when you need it.

Breathe in through your nose to the count of four (1-2-3-4).

Breathe out through your mouth to the count of eight (1-2-3-4-5-6-7-8) while blowing gently, as if you are blowing a bubble. As you do this, imagine that you are blowing away all the anger inside of you. Just let it go.

Breathe in through your nose. Make sure to inhale slowly (1-2-3-4).

Breathe out through your mouth and gently blow away your anger (1-2-3-4-5-6-7-8).

Take another breath in while you count to four (1-2-3-4).

Breathe out to the count of eight (1-2-3-4-5-6-7-8), as if you are blowing a huge bubble.

Breathe in again to the count of four (1-2-3-4) and inhale peace and contentment.

Now breathe out to the count of eight (1-2-3-4-5-6-7-8), imagining you are blowing your anger into a huge bubble.

When the bubble gets so big it pops, let the anger go with it.

Now, breathe normally and pay attention to the bottoms of your feet.

Notice where your feet touch the floor or the ground.

Slowly move your toes; feel your shoes around your feet; notice how your socks feel; notice where the bottoms of your feet touch your shoes and your heels touch the back of your shoes. If you do not have shoes on, feel the floor or ground with the bottoms of your feet.

Keep breathing and focus on the bottoms of your feet until you feel calm.

Practice this mindfulness exercise until you can use it wherever you are and whenever something happens that might lead you to become angry and perhaps lose control. Draw a picture of your feet and hang it where you can see it to remind yourself to use this skill.

You can download an audio recording of this meditation, "Blow Away Anger," at http://www.newharbinger.com/41078.

I Will Think About the Bottoms of My Feet When I Am Angry.

When You Feel Sad

For You to Know

Kids with ADHD sometimes feel sad about how hard it is to remember to do things and to get things done. Or they may feel sad if they get teased or don't have as many friends as they want. You can shift out of a sad feeling by thinking about things that help you feel better.

Daniel often felt sad. He wished he had more friends and felt sad when no one wanted to play with him at recess. He felt sad if he sat alone at lunch. He felt sad when he didn't get invited to a party.

Daniel's therapist helped him understand that it is normal to feel sad sometimes. After he helped Daniel identify things that made him feel sad, he showed Daniel how to replace his sad thoughts with thoughts that made Daniel feel better. Then he taught him how to find something to do that helped him feel less sad. Daniel noticed he felt better after he practiced the skills, because they helped him shift out of a sad feeling.

For You to Do

Write about what was going on when you felt sad.

What was going on when you felt happy?

Draw a picture of yourself feeling happy.

I Feel Happy.

Hang your happy picture where you can see it every day, and remember it any time you feel sad. If you like, you can draw your picture in the "I Feel Happy" worksheet available at http://www.newharbinger.com/41078. This will make it easy to hang your picture anywhere.

More to Do

When you feel sad and want to feel better, you can find a thought that feels better. Here's an example:

> *Sad thought:* I feel sad because no one likes me.
>
> *Thought that feels better:* Sometimes I feel like no one likes me, but my sister likes to play with me, my mom loves me, and yesterday my classmate Sally smiled and said hi to me.

You can also try to think of something to do that will help you feel better.

> *Sad thought:* I feel sad because Sally didn't invite me to her party.
>
> *Thought that helps you change what makes you sad:* I feel sad that I didn't get invited to Sally's party, but I will find something fun to do with my family that day.

Write down two sad thoughts you sometimes have.

Sad thought #1: ____

Sad thought #2: ____

Now, for each thought, write down a thought that feels better than each sad thought. Make sure the thought feels better and you can believe it. Or, write down something you could do that would help you change what makes you sad.

Thought that feels better #1: ______________________________

____

Thought that feels better #2: ______________________________

____

Another way to feel better when you feel sad is to remember something you are thankful for. Here are some examples:

Sad thought: I feel sad because I didn't get the grades I want.

Thankful thought: I am thankful that even though I don't always earn the best grades, I am a good reader and love to read about wonderful adventures.

Sad thought: Sometimes I feel sad because I don't understand how to do my homework.

Thankful thought: Even though my homework is hard, I am thankful that I can ask my teacher for help, stay after school for extra help, or work with my tutor.

Write down a sad thought: ______________________________

Write down a thankful thought related to this sad thought: ______________

____

Draw a picture of something you can remind yourself you are thankful for when you are sad.

I Am Thankful for This.

When You Feel Embarrassed

For You to Know

Sometimes kids with ADHD feel embarrassed when they forget to do something or when they don't finish their schoolwork on time or when they say something without thinking. Being mindful of what makes you feel embarrassed can help you change how you feel.

Madison felt embarrassed when the teacher called on her to answer a question and she didn't know the answer because she had been daydreaming and didn't hear the question. Her face turned red and she felt like sinking into the floor. She wanted to disappear. It seemed like she felt this way almost every day.

Madison made a list of the things that made her feel embarrassed. Then she thought about what she could do differently to prevent those embarrassing situations. For instance, she decided to set the intention to pay attention to what the teacher was asking the class so she would be ready to answer the next time.

She also found it helpful to practice a skill her therapist taught her that she could use to quickly deal with feeling embarrassed.

For You to Do

Write about what was going on when you felt embarrassed.

____

____

____

What did you do to stop feeling embarrassed?

____

____

____

Write about what you could do differently next time to prevent the embarrassing situation in the first place. (For example, set an intention to pay attention to your teacher so you hear questions, and keep bringing your attention back to your teacher as soon as you notice yourself daydreaming. If you don't hear the question, simply ask the teacher to please repeat it for you. Or, remember to calm your body so you don't bump into people while waiting in line.)

____

____

____

More to Do

You can use the following exercise to deal with an embarrassing moment. Read each statement out loud and think about it.

When you feel embarrassed, take a deep breath in and blow it out gently to calm yourself down.

Remind yourself that it's okay, everyone feels embarrassed sometimes.

Avoid drawing attention to yourself by crying, screaming, or storming out of the room.

Admit that you feel embarrassed.

Instead of putting yourself down, see if you can laugh at yourself. Don't take things too seriously.

Explain why you became embarrassed and ask for what you need. This might be as simple as asking the teacher to repeat the question you didn't hear because you were distracted.

Then let it go. It's perfectly okay to make mistakes as long as you learn something that makes it easier to avoid making the same mistake the next time.

To keep from thinking about it over and over, change the channel in your mind from your embarrassed channel to your feel-good channel.

Focus on something you do well for a moment.

Later, when you are calm, think about what it was about the situation that made you feel embarrassed. See if there's anything you can do to keep those things from happening again.

Write down how you will get over feeling embarrassed the next time something happens that embarrasses you.

____

____

You can download an audio recording of this activity, "Get Over an Embarrassing Moment," at http://www.newharbinger.com/41078.

When You Feel Discouraged

For You to Know

Kids with ADHD often get discouraged when they try so hard to do well but don't because they get distracted or forget to do something. They often feel discouraged when they try to make friends and someone doesn't want to be their friend. Noticing when you feel discouraged can help you take action so you can succeed and feel better.

Jayden worked hard to do well in school. Sometimes he felt discouraged when a classmate finished his work before he did. He often felt discouraged when he didn't get as high a score on a test as he expected. He also felt discouraged when it took him longer to get his work done than others because he was easily distracted.

Jayden's ADHD coach helped him explore what happened to make him feel discouraged. He helped Jayden think about what he expected himself to be able to do. With his coach's help Jayden discovered that he put a lot of pressure on himself to succeed, and that he didn't take into account that he had ADHD, which made it hard for him to stay focused and get things done quickly. His coach gave him some questions to ask himself that helped him stop feeling so discouraged.

For You to Do

List three times you felt discouraged.

____

____

____

What helps you feel encouraged?

____

____

____

Write about three things that you felt good about doing this week.

____

____

____

More to Do

When you want to feel less discouraged, consider the following. Ask yourself the questions, and answer them in your head or share your answers with an adult and talk about them.

Don't compare yourself to others.

- Who, if anyone, do I compare myself to?
- What are my positive strengths?

Don't expect too much from yourself.

- What do I expect myself to be able to do that seems hard for me?
- How does ADHD get in the way of me doing well?

Take tiny steps forward.

- When I'm discouraged, what one small thing can I do to get myself feeling better again?

Even when you feel discouraged, there are always good things to notice in the present moment.

- What one good thing can I notice?

Remember some past accomplishments.

- What have I done that pleased me?

Learn and practice how to be more successful.

- What do I need to do differently to do something better? (For example, study and quiz myself until I really know the material, ask my teacher for extra help, get a tutor, ask a teacher or parent about joining a group to learn how to make friends, develop skills to calm my body so I can sit still longer.)

Keep the positive attitude of expecting to be successful.

- How can I practice positive self-talk? (For example, I am learning how to do math; I am smart enough to get a good grade; I am a nice person, so I will be able to find a friend.)

Be willing to do the work you need to do to be successful.

- What do I need to do to be able to do a better job? (For example, I didn't get the grade I wanted because I didn't study enough. Next time I will ask one of my parents to help me study.)

Be willing to ask for help.

- How can I ask for the help I need? (For example, ask for after-school help, ask for more time to take a test, or ask to join a group that teaches people how to make friends.)

Ask yourself positive questions, such as "What do I need to do to get a better grade next time?" or "How can I be a better friend?" (You can download a printable version of this worksheet, "When You Feel Discouraged," at http://www.newharbinger.com/41078.)

Activity 16 When You Feel Stressed

For You to Know

Kids with ADHD often feel stressed-out when things don't go well for them and when they feel overwhelmed and are unable to get everything done that needs to be done. You can learn to calm your mind and body so you feel less stressed. Doing so will help you concentrate better, feel calmer, and do a better job.

Abigail often felt like she wouldn't be able to get all her homework done. She worried that she wouldn't get good grades. Sometimes her stomach hurt when she thought about everything she was supposed to do. She knew she was smart enough to do the work, but it took her longer because she got distracted a lot.

Abigail's therapist explained that it sounded like Abigail was feeling stressed. Abigail felt a little better just knowing that her therapist understood what she was going through. With her therapist's help, Abigail began to notice what was going on when she felt stressed. Then she practiced a Relaxation Breath to calm down and feel better. She loved doing the Body Surfing skill that her therapist taught her as well, and she noticed that her stomach didn't hurt as much when she practiced the skill.

For You to Do

Write about what was going on when you felt stressed.

____

____

____

Draw a picture of something that helps you feel calm when you see it or think about it. If you want, you can use the "I Feel Calm" worksheet to draw your pictures; that way, you can hang this picture where you can see it every day. (You can get the worksheet at http://www.newharbinger.com/41078.) When you feel stressed, imagine the picture in your mind.

I Feel Calm.

You can use the Relaxation Breath to calm your mind and body whenever you feel stressed. Practice doing it three times every day, and then whenever you feel stressed.

Breathe in through your nose as if you are smelling a flower while you count to four (1-2-3-4).

Breathe slowly out through your mouth as if you are blowing a huge bubble while you count to eight (1-2-3-4-5-6-7-8).

Do it again. Breathe in through your nose while you count to four (1-2-3-4), as though you are smelling a flower, and breathe out through your mouth while you count to eight (1-2-3-4-5-6-7-8), while you imagine you are blowing a huge bubble.

One more time. Breathe in calm. Breathe out and relax your mind and body.

Notice how you feel after doing this.

You can download an audio recording of this skill at http://www.newharbinger.com/41078.

More to Do

You can use the Body Surfing skill to calm and center yourself whenever you feel stressed.

Imagine you are surfing a wave of attention that moves through your body.

Start by noticing everything there is to notice about your feet and ankles.

Now pay attention to your legs.

Take a deep breath and imagine you are filling your legs with air.

Now surf to your hips and bottom. Just notice how they feel for a moment.

Ride the wave of attention to your belly and chest. Let them be however they are.

Surf through your back and up to your neck and head. Pay attention to how this part of your body feels.

Bring your attention to your hands and arms.

Take another deep breath and imagine you are filling your whole body with air. As you breathe out, just let everything go that needs to go.

How does your body feel now that you are done body surfing?

You can download an audio recording of this skill at http://www.newharbinger.com/41078.

How Does Your Body Feel? Activity 17

For You to Know

Kids with ADHD may feel stressed and worried as they struggle to concentrate and do well in school, at home, in after-school activities, and while hanging out with friends. Taking a few minutes to pay attention to your body when you're stressed will help you tune in to what is going on in your body. Then you can do what you need to do to take good care of yourself.

Christopher often forgot to eat because he didn't notice that he was hungry while doing schoolwork or playing. Sometimes he played outside without his coat even though he was shivering. And the other day he didn't notice he had to go to the restroom until it was almost too late. Sometimes his stomach hurt and he didn't know why.

Christopher's therapist explained that it sounded like he was not aware of how his body felt. She asked him to draw some pictures that helped him tune in to how his body was feeling. He had trouble at first, but with practice he got better at noticing when he was hungry, warm, hyperactive, tense, or tired, and also when his mind was clear or cloudy. By tuning in to his body, he could do what he needed to do to take care of himself, such as eat, put on a coat, calm down his worry, relax his body, or rest.

For You to Do

Use the following activity to practice tuning in to how your body feels.

Draw pictures of each item, and tune in to your body and notice how you feel now. Then place an *X* on the number that matches how you feel. For example, if you are really hot (like a hot potato), place an *X* on the number 5. If you're freezing, place an *X* on the number 1. If you are not really hot nor really cold, place an *X* on the number 3.

How warm do you feel?

Cold: Draw an ice cube.

1—2—3—4—5

Hot: Draw a hot baked potato.

How hungry do you feel?

1—2—3—4—5

Empty: Draw an empty glass.

Full: Draw a full glass.

How active is your body?

1—2—3—4—5

Still: Draw a sleeping dog.

Active: Draw a hopping rabbit.

How tight are your muscles?

1—2—3—4—5

Relaxed: Draw a limp piece of spaghetti.

Tight: Draw a knot in a rope.

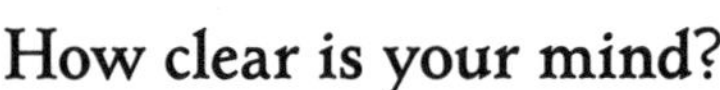

How clear is your mind?

1—2—3—4—5

Cloudy: Draw a cloudy sky.

Clear: Draw a clear sky.

How awake are you?

1—2—3—4—5

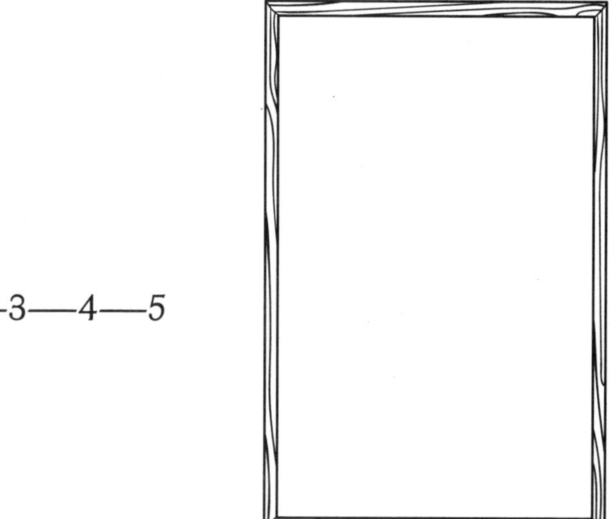

Tired: Draw someone sleeping.

Wide Awake: Draw a runner.

More to Do

Draw a happy face on the lines above to mark how you like to feel.

Example: 1—2—3—4—5

At least once every day, stop for a moment and tune in to your body. Then you can do what you need to do to take care of yourself. For example, if you are hungry, eat; put a coat on when you are cold; if you're hyperactive, calm your body; rest when you are tired.

Activity 18 Calming Your Busy Body

For You to Know

Many kids with ADHD are constantly moving their bodies. They have trouble sitting still and keeping their body calm. When you notice yourself moving a lot, you can use mindfulness to calm your body and keep it still.

Noah was always moving. His parents were always saying, "Sit still, Noah." His teacher yelled at him when he got out of his seat. Even his friends were sometimes annoyed with him when he fidgeted and talked nonstop.

Noah's therapist showed him how to be aware that his body was moving a lot and taught him how to calm his body and practice sitting still. After learning these skills, Noah still moved a lot, but he could sit still for longer periods of time when he really needed to.

For You to Do

Constantly moving is a common sign of ADHD and is called hyperactivity. The first step in controlling hyperactivity is to become aware of it.

Here are some of the things people do or experience when they're hyperactive. Place checkmarks next to the behaviors you notice yourself doing, or ways that you feel.

Also, ask your parents, friends, and teachers if they have noticed you doing any of the listed behaviors.

- ☐ Constantly moving
- ☐ Fidgeting
- ☐ Finger tapping
- ☐ Foot tapping
- ☐ Leg swinging
- ☐ Having trouble sitting still
- ☐ Having lots of energy
- ☐ Restlessness
- ☐ Talking too much
- ☐ Pacing
- ☐ Can't relax
- ☐ Feeling wired

Practice sitting still by playing the Freeze Dust game so you can calm your body down when you're feeling wired or restless or any of the other things listed above.

1. Imagine that you have been sprinkled with freeze dust, which freezes your body in place.
2. Pretend you are frozen in place and are sitting as still as a statue.
3. Keep breathing.
4. Pay attention to your breath and see how long you can stay frozen.
5. Notice the stillness in your body.
6. Ask someone to time you, and see if you can stay frozen longer with practice.
7. Any time during the day that you notice you are moving too much, remember what it felt like to "freeze" and quickly bring your body to stillness.

More to Do

Practice playing the Balancing Chips game to teach yourself to lie still. The game will help you notice your body and practice keeping it still.

1. Collect about seven to eight coins or chips from a board game.
2. Lie down on your back.
3. One by one, place the coins or chips on your legs, shoulders, forehead, and chin. Ask someone to help you, if you need it.
4. Now pay attention to how the coins or chips feel as you lie still and balance them on your body.
5. See how long you can lie still before you move and knock them off.

Practice this every day and notice if you can lie still a little longer each time.

If you have trouble sitting still during the day, close your eyes for a moment and imagine how it felt when you were balancing the coins or chips. Notice if doing this helps you calm your body.

For further practice with tuning in and calming your body, you can download a script and an audio recording of the "Calming Your Busy Body" meditation at http://www.newharbinger.com/41078. Listen to the recording or read the script whenever you feel hyper; eventually you'll be able to do the meditation on your own to calm your body whenever you need to.

Quieting Your Inner Critic Activity 19

For You to Know

ADHD can sometimes make you feel bad about yourself. Even when you try so hard to do everything right, you may get distracted, forget to do things, and not get things done on time. Then a little voice inside you might criticize you and say mean things. This is your Inner Critic. You can feel better when you learn how to quiet your Inner Critic.

Chloe often put herself down. She sometimes called herself stupid in her head. She would even tell herself, You can't do that, so don't even try.

Chloe's therapist explained that sometimes we talk to ourselves and have conversations inside our heads that can be critical of us and make us feel bad. She asked Chloe to notice what her Inner Critic said to her. Chloe noticed that sometimes her Inner Critic was mean to her and said things Chloe would never say to anyone else. Chloe practiced talking back to her Inner Critic and rewriting its unhelpful statements as ones that felt better. She noticed her Inner Critic was quieter and less mean after she learned that skill. And Chloe found that her Inner Critic's words didn't stop her as often from trying hard to accomplish goals.

For You to Do

Let's find out if you have an Inner Critic who says mean and unhelpful things to you. Notice what you say to yourself or what your inner voice inside your head says. Write down three things you noticed.

1. ______________________________

2. ______________________________

3. ______________________________

For any of the three things you listed that were unhelpful, mean, or made you feel bad, write a more helpful statement. For example, if your Inner Critic says *You are stupid*, you can talk back like this: "Yes, Inner Critic, sometimes I feel stupid, but I am not stupid. I'm actually pretty smart about some things." If your Inner Critic says *You will never get this done in time*, you can rewrite this statement as, "Yes, Inner Critic, I worry that I won't get done in time, but I am breathing slowly to calm myself down, and I'm keeping my attention on my work until it is done."

1. ______________________________

2. ______________________________

3. ______________________________

More to Do

Use the following Quieting Your Inner Critic practice to have a conversation with your Inner Critic and change its critical or unhelpful statements to more positive and helpful self-statements. Practice this process whenever you notice your Inner Critic is being critical or making you feel bad.

> Sit quietly and take a deep breath in through your nose and gently blow the air out through your mouth.
>
> Notice what your inner voice says to you.
>
> Is what it says to you kind enough that you would say it to a friend?
>
> Is the voice an Inner Critic? Does what it says make you feel bad; put you down; tell you that you are not good enough, are wrong, are stupid, or can't do something?
>
> If your inner voice is an Inner Critic:
>
>> Talk back to your inner voice. For example, "You are making me feel bad, Inner Critic. Please don't talk to me that way. I know you are probably trying to help me do a good job, but I don't need your help right now. Thanks for trying to help me. I know the mean things you say aren't true, even if they seem like they are."
>>
>> Change what the Inner Critic says to a kinder self-statement. For example, "Although I didn't know the answer in class today, I will work with my teacher to make sure I learn what I need to know." Make sure your new self-statement makes you feel better and is believable.
>>
>> Notice how you feel with the kinder, more helpful statements.

You can download an audio recording of this meditation, "Quieting Your Inner Critic," at http://www.newharbinger.com/41078.

What Do You Like About Yourself?

For You to Know

Sometimes kids with ADHD feel bad about themselves. By paying attention to things that you like about yourself, you can feel better.

Anthony often thought about the things he didn't like about himself. He felt bad when he thought about his grades and how often he lost things he needed. He didn't like how uncomfortable he felt when he tried to make friends.

Anthony made a list of things that he liked about himself. He was surprised to see that there were lots of things he liked about himself. This made him feel much better.

For You to Do

Write down three things you like about yourself. Here are some examples: I have lots of energy, I'm kind, I have lots of ideas, I am fun, I can run fast, I help my mom, I can read.

____

____

____

What Do You Like About Yourself? Activity 20

Ask your parents to write down three things they like about you.

1. ______________________________

2. ______________________________

3. ______________________________

Ask your favorite teacher to write down three things he or she likes about you.

1. ______________________________

2. ______________________________

3. ______________________________

Write down three things you enjoy doing.

1. ______________________________

2. ______________________________

3. ______________________________

Write down three things you do well.

1. ______________________________

2. ______________________________

3. ______________________________

Write down three things your friends or classmates or siblings like about you.

1. ______________________________

2. ______________________________

3. ______________________________

Write down three things you like about your body.

1. ______________________________

2. ______________________________

3. ______________________________

Write down three things you like about helping others.

1. ______________________________

2. ______________________________

3. ______________________________

Write down three things you learned to do.

1. ______________________________

2. ______________________________

3. ______________________________

Write down three kind things you said to someone else.

1. ______________________________

2. ______________________________

3. ______________________________

Write down three kind things you did.

1. ______________________________

2. ______________________________

3. ______________________________

Write down three things you are proud of.

1. ______________________________

2. ______________________________

3. ______________________________

Write down three things you are glad you did.

1. ______________________________

2. ______________________________

3. ______________________________

Post this list where you can see it every day. Whenever you feel discouraged or embarrassed, read it out loud to help yourself feel better. When you have done this for a few weeks, start adding things you like about yourself to the list. You can download a printable version of this worksheet, "What I Like About Myself," at http://www.newharbinger.com/41078. It might make your list easier to post.

Section 4

Mindfulness of Healthy Choices

Kids with ADHD perform better when they get enough sleep, eat well, and make good choices about food, exercise, and screen time. This section of the book will show you ways to get the sleep you need to do your best. It will also help you be mindful of what and when you eat, how much exercise you get, and how much time you spend in front of a screen, such as a computer or tablet.

Activity 21

How Much Sleep Do You Need?

For You to Know

Often ADHD makes it hard to get enough sleep. You may stay up too late or have trouble falling asleep or getting up on time. ADHD symptoms tend to be much worse when you don't sleep enough. Figuring out how much sleep you need every night to do your best during the day can help you get the sleep you need and concentrate better during the day.

Alden felt tired a lot. Sometimes he even fell asleep in class. He felt so embarrassed when his teacher asked him if she was "keeping him up" and his classmates all laughed at him.

He didn't know why he was so tired, but when he learned how much sleep he needed to feel good he realized that most nights he wasn't getting enough sleep. He was surprised to find out that kids his age need ten to eleven hours each night—and sometimes more!

He figured out what time he needed to go to bed each night so he could get enough sleep. He felt much better, and his concentration during the day improved when he got enough sleep.

For You to Do

Think about what symptoms make you know you are tired. Circle all the signs you notice in yourself.

- You feel tired.
- You fall asleep during the day, in class, while reading, while riding in the car, or while watching a show.
- You have more trouble concentrating.
- You fidget and have more trouble sitting still.
- You feel cranky and grumpy.
- You are easily annoyed and quickly frustrated.
- You have trouble getting yourself to do things.
- You don't feel like doing things you usually enjoy.
- You don't have enough energy.
- Other: ____

Fill out this Sleep Diary to figure out how much sleep makes you feel the best. Ask an adult for help, if you need it. Fill in what time you went to bed, fell asleep, and woke up the next day. Rate how tired you were the next day on a scale of 0 to 5, where 0 is not tired at all and 5 is very tired. (You can download a printable version of this diary at http://www.newharbinger.com/41078.)

Day	*Went to Bed*	*Went to Sleep (Estimated)*	*Woke Up*	*(A) Total Hours Slept*	*(B) Tiredness Rating the Next Day (0–5)*
Monday					
Tuesday					
Wednesday					
Thursday					
Friday					
Saturday					
Sunday					

More to Do

Now, let's use the Sleep Diary to figure out how much sleep you need.

1. What's the most sleep you got? (See column A.) ______________
2. On a scale of 0 to 5, how tired were you when you slept this much? (See column B.) ______________
3. What's the least amount of sleep you got? (See column A.) ______________
4. On a scale of 0 to 5, how tired were you when you slept this much? (See column B.) ______________
5. How many hours of sleep per night made you feel the best? ______________

Now let's figure out your ideal bedtime.

1. What time do you have to get up in the morning? ______________
2. How many hours of sleep do you need to feel your best? (See number 5 above.): ______________
3. To figure out your ideal bedtime, subtract the number of hours of sleep you need from the time you have to get up. ______________

Example:

1. You need to get up at 6:30 a.m.
2. You need 10.5 hours of sleep.
3. Your bedtime is: 6:30 a.m. – 10.5 hours = 8:00 p.m.

Activity 22 Getting to Bed on Time

For You to Know

Sometimes kids with ADHD have trouble getting to bed on time. Often they get busy doing something and don't notice that it is time for bed. Then they feel tired and more distracted the next day. Following a bedtime routine can help you get to bed on time.

Even though Addison knew what her bedtime was, she often got distracted and forgot to notice what time it was and then stayed up way too late. The next day she was tired, was grumpy, and had more trouble than usual paying attention in school.

Addison learned to mindfully set an intention to go to bed at the same time every night. She created a bedtime routine map that helped her get things done in time for bed. She also learned how to get ready for sleep. At first it was hard to follow the new bedtime routine. But she noticed that after about two weeks it was really easy, and she got to bed on time almost every night.

For You to Do

You can get to bed on time when you follow the same routine each night. Let's create a Bedtime Routine Map.

On the following Bedtime Routine Map worksheet, put a star by each picture showing something you need to do before bed. If there is anything else you need to do that isn't shown, draw a picture of it in the blank circles labeled "other" and write what the activity is below. Draw an *X* through any of the pictures that show activities you don't need to do.

Then pretend you are doing the things you need to do to get to bed on time. Think about what you need to do first and put the number 1 by that picture. Then put the number 2 on the next thing you need to do. Keep going until you have numbered all the pictures that you put a star next to or drew. An example order might be (1) homework, (2) chores, (3) play, (4) pack backpack, (5) get clothes ready, (6) brush teeth and wash face, (7) read, (8) listen to sleep meditation, (9) go to sleep.

Starting at the first thing you need to do, draw a line to the next task, and so on, ending the line with you asleep in bed. This will be your map to follow each night to make sure you get everything done and get to bed on time.

Remember to post your Bedtime Routine Map where you can see it. You can download a printable version of this worksheet at http://www.newharbinger.com/41078.

Bedtime Routine Map

More to Do

You will be able to get to bed on time and fall asleep faster if you get ready to go to sleep. The following "Get Ready to Sleep" checklist includes important things you can do to make sure your brain and body are ready to sleep. Review it at dinnertime each night for a week. Fill in the times requested and check off each item as you do them. (You can download a printable version of this checklist at http://www.newharbinger.com/41078.)

- ☐ I will go to bed at my ideal bedtime, which is (see activity 21): ________________
- ☐ I will calm my brain and body by:
  - ☐ Turning off the TV at least one hour before bedtime.
  - ☐ Stopping activities that keep my brain awake at least an hour before bedtime. This includes sports, games, hobbies, texting, and using the computer, tablet, or phone.
  - ☐ Stopping exercise at least two hours before bedtime.
  - ☐ Reading (dim the brightness when using tablets).
  - ☐ Listening to quiet music.
  - ☐ Listening to a sleep meditation. (You can download a script and an audio recording of "Sleep Meditation to Calm Your Mind and Body" at http://www.newharbinger.com/41078.)
- ☐ I will make sure my bedroom is comfortable and quiet by:
  - ☐ Turning down lights a half hour before bedtime.
  - ☐ Closing the shades to keep my bedroom dark.
  - ☐ Turning off noise-producing devices or using a sound machine to mask noise that I can't turn off.
  - ☐ Wearing comfortable sleeping clothes.
  - ☐ Making sure my bed is comfy.
- ☐ I will set an alarm that repeats every night to remind myself to get ready for bed.

Activity 23 Paying Attention When You Are Eating

For You to Know

Kids with ADHD need a healthy diet to keep their brain and body healthy. When you are mindful about choosing foods that your brain and body need to work their best, as well as paying attention to eating when you are eating, you will ensure that your diet is nutritious and healthy.

Alexis, an eight-year-old girl with ADHD, often felt either wired and hyperactive or worn out, tired, and unfocused. She didn't understand how she could feel full of energy one minute and then have no energy a few minutes later. Even her ability to concentrate changed from moment to moment.

When she learned that food could be affecting her energy and focus, she started being mindful of what she was eating, choosing to eat helpful foods and limiting unhelpful foods. She noticed that when she ate breakfast, lunch, and dinner instead of skipping meals she felt better and her concentration improved. Her energy and focus improved even more when she chose helpful foods such as fruits, veggies, eggs, lean meat and fish, and nuts instead of foods full of sugar or caffeine, such as soda and cookies.

For You to Do

Certain foods can make ADHD symptoms worse for some kids. Next time you notice that you are either hyper, distracted, and revved up or tired, unfocused, and not feeling like doing anything, think about what food you ate that day. Coffee and many sodas and energy drinks contain caffeine. Caffeine and sugary foods may give you lots of energy right away but then quickly leave you without enough energy.

Here are lists of some helpful and unhelpful foods. Circle the foods that you ate today.

Helpful Foods	**Unhelpful Foods**
Fruit	Sugar and corn syrup
Vegetables	Candy
Nuts and seeds	Cookies
Whole grains	Cake
Milk and cheese	Soda
Fish	Caffeine
Chicken and turkey	Potato chips
Lean beef	Sugary cereals

Next time you are about to eat something, stop and think about which list that food is on. Is it on the helpful or unhelpful list? Be mindful about the foods you eat, and choose foods that are on the helpful list.

More to Do

When you eat mindfully you bring your attention to the present moment, notice and enjoy what you eat, become aware of when you are full, and make better food choices. First try the following practice in your imagination, and then use it for a few minutes each time you eat.

Close your eyes and pretend that you are eating a grape.

Set the intention to pay attention to everything there is to notice about eating the grape.

Whenever thoughts arise that are not about eating the grape, notice them, let them go, and remind yourself of your intention to pay attention to the grape.

Imagine you are looking at the grape. Is the grape on the helpful or unhelpful foods list?

Notice how the grape looks.

What color is it?

What shape is it?

Roll it in your fingers. How does it feel? Is it warm or cool? Is it hard or squishy? Is it heavy or light?

Take a sniff and notice what the grape smells like.

Before you start to eat the grape, pay attention to how your stomach feels. Does it feel full or empty? Is it comfortable or uncomfortable? Can you connect how it feels with hunger? Make sure you are hungry before you eat.

Place the grape in your mouth but don't chew or swallow it yet. Notice if it is warm or cold. How does it feel in your mouth, on your tongue, and on your teeth?

Take a bite and pay attention to how it feels when you chew the grape. Focus on the flavor and the texture. Is it crunchy, chewy, soft, or hard? Notice if it is slippery, smooth, rough, sweet, or sour. Be aware of whether it sticks to your teeth.

If your mind wanders, that's okay. Just remember your intention and bring your attention back to eating.

Again, notice the feeling of the grape in your mouth, on your teeth, on your tongue, on your lips.

Chew until the grape is completely ready to be swallowed.

Swallow. Pay attention to how the grape feels as it leaves your mouth and slides down your throat. Notice how far down it goes before you can't feel it anymore. Notice if there is any food still in your mouth or if it's empty now.

Tune in to how your stomach feels. Notice how it feels different after you have eaten a little food and then after you have eaten a lot of food.

Use this process when you are actually eating, and repeat it until your food is gone or until you feel full.

You can download an audio recording of this meditation, "Mindful Eating," at http://www.newharbinger.com/41078.

Getting Enough Exercise

For You to Know

Getting regular exercise and moving the body can help kids with ADHD to concentrate, to calm their busy body, and to do better in school. You can find ways to move your body every day.

Mia had ADHD and often had trouble sitting still. Plus her mind wandered a lot. The longer she sat at her desk trying to pay attention, the harder it got. She always felt like she needed to move.

She noticed that she could sit still more easily and pay attention to her schoolwork much better right after she had run around and played games during recess. So she started making sure she got exercise every day. She even started playing basketball, which helped her burn off her extra energy.

When she got enough exercise, her parents and her teacher told her she was calmer and more focused. She could always tell when she didn't get enough exercise, because her body felt like it was bursting with energy and she couldn't sit and focus for very long.

For You to Do

Write about the exercise you got this week. Include what you did, how often, and for how long.

____

____

____

Draw a picture of yourself getting exercise or playing your favorite sport (or one you would like to play). Exercise might include walking, running, bicycling, dancing, jumping rope, swimming, paddling, playing tag, or playing ball.

I Am Getting Some Exercise.

How does getting exercise help you pay attention or calm your body, or both?

___

___

___

Write about how you can get more exercise every day.

___

___

___

More to Do

Mindful Movement can help you get exercise, improve your concentration, and calm your body.

Mindful Movement #1

1. Stand up.
2. Place your hands at your sides with your arms straight.
3. Breathe in and raise your arms up over your head to touch the sky while counting to four (1-2-3-4).
4. Breathe out and lower your arms slowly while counting to eight (1-2-3-4-5-6-7-8).
5. Repeat steps 2 through 4 three more times.

Mindful Movement #2

1. Stand up straight.
2. Bend at the waist, and reach down and touch the floor while you breathe out. Notice how close your hands come to the floor. Can you touch the floor without bending your knees?
3. Stand back up while you breathe in. Notice how your body feels when you stand up straight.
4. Bend over, and reach down and touch the floor while you breathe out. Pay attention to how your body feels bending over like this.
5. Stand up while you breathe in.
6. Do it again. Reach down and touch the floor while you breathe out.
7. Stand up while you breathe in. Notice how fast your heart is beating.

Use your imagination to create two more Mindful Movements you can do with your body, describe them here, and practice them.

____

____

____

____

Activity 25

Spending Time Outdoors in Nature

For You to Know

Spending time outdoors where there are trees, grass, flowers, and plants can help kids with ADHD concentrate and sit still longer. You can find ways to spend time outdoors every day. Being mindful of your surroundings while you are outdoors will help you enjoy nature and concentrate even better when you need to.

Christopher loved to be outdoors. When he had trouble sitting still in school he often looked out the window and daydreamed about being outdoors. He loved to lie on his back and find clouds whose shapes looked like something, such as an animal. He loved going for long walks and noticing the trees and squirrels. Sometimes he helped his mother work in the garden. When he visited his cousin in the city, they played in the local park.

Christopher knew that spending time outdoors helped him pay attention in school. His body felt calmer after he spent time outside, and he could get his schoolwork done faster. On days when he couldn't be outdoors, he found that it helped to imagine he was outdoors using a meditation his therapist taught him.

For You to Do

Draw a picture of yourself spending time outdoors. Include where you were, what the weather was like, and whether you were surrounded by cars and buildings or trees, grass, flowers, or water—or perhaps all of these things.

I Am Outdoors.

What do you like best about being outdoors?

____

____

____

How do you feel when you are outdoors?

____

____

____

Does spending time outdoors help you sit still and concentrate when you need to, and if yes, how?

____

____

____

What time can you spend outdoors every day, even if for only thirty minutes?

____

____

____

More to Do

Paying attention to everything around you while outdoors is a great way to practice mindfulness and to enjoy being outside. You can practice mindfulness while going for a walk, which is a great activity if you have trouble sitting still.

If possible, go outdoors to do this Mindfulness of Surroundings in Nature meditation. If that's not possible, try closing your eyes and imagining you are outdoors someplace you've been or seen in a video.

Let's begin.

Look at your surroundings and see what's around you.

Can you see some trees? If so, look closely at one of the trees. Is the tree perfectly still or is it moving in the breeze? Does it have leaves or are the branches bare? What color are the leaves or the branches? Are there buds on the branches, or flowers? Does the tree have needles and pinecones?

Look up at the sky. What color is it? Is it clear or cloudy? What do the clouds look like?

Is the sun shining or hidden behind clouds?

Take a breath in and notice what you smell. Is there a fragrance or odor? Where is it coming from?

Is there grass? What color is it? Is it healthy and green or dried out and brown? Is it long or neatly mowed? If you can, reach down and touch the grass. What does it feel like?

Can you see flowers? Notice their colors and shapes. Smell them if you can.

Are there any rocks in view? Look at their shape and color. Touch them and notice how they feel.

Can you see a lake or the ocean? Pay attention to the water. Is it calm and still or moving and full of waves? What color is it?

Do you see any animals?

Stop and listen. What do you hear? Are there birds singing? Can you hear the wind blowing in the trees? Is there sound from a stream or a waterfall or the ocean surf? Do you hear the sounds of cars, trucks, planes, motors, horns, or sirens?

How warm is it? Is the air still or is there a breeze, or perhaps a strong wind?

Now that you have spent some time paying attention to your natural surroundings, bring your awareness with you as you go back to your daily activities.

You can practice this skill every time you are outdoors or by using your imagination to pretend you are outdoors.

You can download an audio recording of this meditation at http://www.newharbinger.com/41078.

Using Screen Time in a Healthy Way

For You to Know

Kids use screens every day on computers, tablets, video games, smartphones, and TVs. Using a screen to learn something new or to play a game for a little while can be educational and fun. But sometimes kids use screens for many hours a day when they could or should be doing something else. You can figure out if you use screens too much, and if you do you can find ways to reduce your use.

David loved to play games on his tablet. He would rather play games than do anything else, including playing with friends or doing other things he used to enjoy. He often played for hours and forgot to do his homework and chores. He wouldn't notice his mother reminding him to shut off the games and do his homework until she yelled at him—really loudly.

David's mother told him she felt that he was playing his games too much. She said screen time was getting in the way of him doing what he was supposed to do and of enjoying other things in life. She helped David create a plan to use his screens in a healthier way. David found that he was glad that he could get his chores and homework done, have fun with his friends, do some of his favorite hobbies, and still have some screen time to play his games.

For You to Do

Draw a picture of all the screens (computer, tablet, smartphone, video games, TV) you use.

What do you use them for? (For example, to do homework, to connect with friends, to play games, to surf the Internet, to watch movies or TV.)

___

___

Are you using screens too much? Check all examples that apply.

- ☐ You would rather use screens than do other things.
- ☐ When asked to turn the screens off, you get angry or have a temper tantrum.
- ☐ You agree to turn them off but then don't.
- ☐ You stay up past your bedtime using them.
- ☐ You neglect your chores, homework, or friends in favor of using them.
- ☐ You use screens for more than two hours per day total.

If you checked off any of the statements above, screen time may be getting in the way of you doing what you need to do. The next part of this activity could help.

More to Do

Some kids who struggle with screen time set an alarm to remind themselves when it should end. You could also make sure you've finished homework before you play games or use social media. You might choose not to use screens after a certain time at night, make time to do things you enjoy besides screen time, or set and follow a schedule for screen time. How can you limit your screen time? Write your thoughts here.

___

___

___

Circle fun things you can do instead of screen time.

Play outdoors	Learn to sing or play an instrument
Read	Play with a friend
Hobbies	Use my imagination in free play
Crafts	Play dress up
Sports	Draw or paint
Listen to music	Write a story

Meditation Time

For You to Know

Kids with ADHD often have very busy brains that think all the time without stopping. This can make you bright and smart, but sometimes brains need to quiet down and rest, especially the brains of people who get distracted easily or daydream a lot. You can learn to quiet your brain by doing a short meditation during which you pay attention to your breath.

Ella had a very busy brain. She was always thinking about something, and she daydreamed a lot. Sometimes she had trouble calming her brain enough to focus on her schoolwork. Often she felt like she had no control over her thoughts. She wished she could keep her mind focused on what she needed to do.

Ella's therapist taught her how to do the Core Mindfulness Meditation in which she focused on her breath. When Ella first started practicing, she worried that she would never be able to calm her thoughts enough to stay focused on her breath. But she stuck with the meditation and practiced at least once every day. Every time she noticed that her mind was no longer focused on her breath, she simply let go of the thought and brought her attention back to her breath. After about two weeks she noticed that it was easier to stay focused, not only while doing the meditation but also while doing schoolwork.

For You to Do

Draw a picture of your brain full of busy thoughts.

Draw a picture of your brain paying attention to one thought.

More to Do

It is normal for thoughts to wander, but you can train your brain to calm down while you focus on your breath. Then you will find it easier to focus on things you need to do, such as schoolwork. Calming and focusing your brain will get easier the more you do it. The following Core Mindfulness Meditation is good for focusing the mind.

Set your intention to focus on your breath.

Pay attention to your breath.

As soon as you notice that you are thinking about something besides your breath, just let go of the thought and bring your attention back to your breath.

Do this over and over and over. Start with thirty seconds, and then increase your practice by thirty seconds until you can do it for five minutes at a time.

You can download a complete "Core Mindfulness Meditation" script and audio recording at http://www.newharbinger.com/41078.

Section 5

Mindfulness at School

This part of the book provides mindfulness skills that will help you organize your space and your schoolwork, get things done faster, improve your concentration, take tests with less worry, sit still longer, keep track of your things, and succeed more easily in school.

Activity 28

How Long Can You Pay Attention?

For You to Know

Having ADHD can make it harder to stay on task and finish schoolwork on time. When you know how long you can pay attention, you can break your schoolwork into smaller chunks that better match your attention span. Approaching your work this way will make it easier to stay on task and get things done.

Andrew had trouble concentrating. He could stay focused for a little while but then it got harder and harder to focus. Soon his mind was wandering all over the place. He often forgot what he was doing. It seemed to take forever to get his homework done.

After Andrew figured out how long he could pay attention, he used a timer to break tasks into smaller pieces that took about as long as he could easily pay attention. When he heard the timer alarm, it brought his attention back to what he was supposed to be paying attention to. Using this skill, he noticed that he was getting things done faster.

For You to Do

Let's find out how long you can concentrate. Ask an adult for help, if you need it. Pick a task, such as reading or doing homework or a fun project, and follow these instructions:

1. Start a stopwatch.
2. Pay attention to your book, homework, or project. As soon as you notice that you are distracted and no longer paying attention, stop the stopwatch.
3. Write down the time on the stopwatch, which is how long you were able to pay attention.
4. Do steps 1 through 3 ten times.
5. Use your math skills to convert all the times you wrote down to seconds.
6. Add up all the times you wrote down and divide by ten.
7. Divide by sixty to convert seconds back to minutes.
8. This figure is the average length of time you paid attention over ten trials.

Write down the average time you can concentrate: ______________________________

More to Do

Now that you know how long you can pay attention, break your work into chunks that take about that long. Then follow this procedure:

1. Set a timer for the average time you can concentrate.
2. Pay attention to your task.
3. When the timer alarm sounds, take a short break. Stretch your arms over your head for a moment, and then restart the timer.
4. Bring your attention back to your task.
5. Repeat steps 2 through 4 until you finish your task.

Sometimes your attention span will improve if you let yourself daydream on purpose. To try this out, download the bonus activity "Daydreaming on Purpose" at http://www.newharbinger.com/41078.

You Can Pay Attention Longer

For You to Know

ADHD makes it hard to pay attention. You can learn to pay attention longer when you remove things that distract you, practice noticing when you are distracted, and bring your attention back to your task—over and over again. Doing these things will teach your brain to pay attention a bit longer.

Lots of things distracted Andrew. It took him a long time to get things done. He would sit down to do his homework and start playing with the paperclips on his desk. Or he would start to read a book and get up to play with his dog. Sometimes his own thoughts distracted him, and he would forget to pay attention to his schoolwork. When he ate a lot of sugar or didn't get a good night's sleep, he had even more trouble paying attention.

When Andrew became mindful about what usually distracted him, he found ways to remove or avoid it. He also used a meditation that helped him practice bringing his attention back to his homework over and over. Using these skills he noticed that he was able to pay attention for longer periods of time, and that when he got distracted he could get himself back on task more quickly.

For You to Do

Your ability to pay attention may depend on what's going on inside you. Circle things that make it harder for you to pay attention.

Feeling tired

Worrying

Feeling sad

Being angry

Being frustrated

Feeling hungry

Being stressed

Eating sugar

Lots of things around you can distract you. Draw a picture of three things that distract you. Examples include the phone, TV, the radio, friends talking, noise, daydreaming, people walking by, toys, pets, touching things, and itchy clothes.

This Distracts Me.

Now that you are mindful of what distracts you, write a sentence to describe what you can do to help yourself concentrate. Examples include getting a good night's sleep; putting the dog out when you do homework; turning off the phone, TV, or radio; calming yourself; removing itchy tags from clothes; and avoiding sugary snacks.

____

____

____

More to Do

Read or listen to the following Mindfulness of Tasks While Doing Homework meditation to practice bringing your attention back to your homework. Then remember to do this practice when you do your homework.

Close your eyes and use your imagination to practice doing your homework.

Set the intention to pay attention to your homework until it is done.

Pay attention to your homework.

Feel the book, pencil, or keyboard with your fingers.

Notice what you are learning about or the problem you are trying to solve.

Pay attention to where to find the answers you need to complete your homework.

Notice how your fingers feel as they write down or type the answer.

Notice how your brain feels when you learn something new or you know the answer.

If you are reading a book, pay attention to the story, the characters and their conversation, and the images in your head that form when you read.

When you notice you are distracted and thinking about something besides your homework, let go of the distracted thought and bring your attention back to the homework.

It is normal to be distracted. Just remember to bring your attention back to your homework as soon as you notice you are distracted.

Do this over and over again until your homework is done.

Whenever you do your homework or work on a project, remind yourself to do this practice to pay attention longer. You can download an audio recording of the "Mindfulness of Tasks While Doing Homework" meditation at http://www.newharbinger.com/41078.

Keeping Track of Your Schoolwork

For You to Know

ADHD can make it hard to organize your schoolwork. When you know what the assignments are, you will know what you need to do and when. When you use a system to keep your school papers organized, you will do better in school.

Samantha was a smart ten-year-old, but her grades didn't show it. They were low because she had trouble getting her homework done and turned in. Sometimes she didn't know what the assignment was. Sometimes she did the homework and then lost it before she turned it in. She got so far behind that she felt she would never catch up.

Once she set her intention to get her homework turned in, she started using a system that her teacher showed her to help her keep track of her assignments and to organize her homework. She felt better when she started getting full credit for her homework, and she found that she understood her schoolwork better after doing her homework.

For You to Do

Let's find out if you have trouble organizing your schoolwork. If you check off any of the listed items, you do.

- ☐ I often don't know what my assignments are.
- ☐ I forget to write down homework assignments and when they are due.
- ☐ I fall behind on my homework.
- ☐ I get lower grades because I don't turn my homework in.
- ☐ I often lose my homework, even after I complete it.
- ☐ I worry about school because I am behind.

You can use mindfulness and organizational skills to make sure you know what your homework assignment is and when it is due. Read the following steps out loud, and then practice doing each step until it becomes a habit. Check them off as you do them. You'll notice how much easier it is to get your homework done when you know what the assignment is.

- ☐ I will find a way to keep track of what my assignments are and when they are due by:
  - ☐ Asking my teacher for help.
  - ☐ Searching online for a homework app I can use on my smartphone or tablet.
  - ☐ Finding and using an assignment book.
  - ☐ Seeing if assignments are available online at my school's website.

- ☐ Before I leave each class I will write down or enter my assignments and when they are due. If I often forget to do this, I will ask the teacher for help or set an alarm on my smartphone to remind me.
- ☐ I will break large homework projects into small pieces and enter in my assignment book or app when I should have each piece done.
- ☐ I will look at my assignments each day to remind myself what I need to do.

More to Do

Another strategy to succeed at getting your homework done on time and turning it in is to use a folder system. You can use colored folders that have pockets inside each cover to keep track of homework as it's assigned and when you've completed it. Read through the steps below. Then check them off as you practice doing them until they become a habit. You'll find it's much easier to keep your homework organized when you follow these steps.

- ☐ I will use colored folders that have pockets inside each cover, one for each class.
- ☐ When a homework paper is assigned, I will place it in the right-hand pocket of the folder for that class.
- ☐ When I sit down to do my homework, I will look at my assignments and when they are due, and I will work on the homework that is due first before moving on to other assignments.
- ☐ I will take out the books or papers, or both, that I need for that particular homework.

- [ ] I will do the homework for one class at a time, and when I am done I will put the homework to be turned in inside the left-hand pocket of the colored folder for that class.
- [ ] I will keep all the folders in a "homework" binder.
- [ ] When all my homework is done, I will place my folders and homework binder where it belongs in my backpack and place the backpack by the door before I go to bed so I will see it and remember to take it to school.
- [ ] I will place graded homework in a separate folder, one for each class, so I can refer to it when I study.
- [ ] **Bonus step:** I will ask my parent to ask my school for a second set of textbooks that I can keep at home so I always have the books I need.

You can download a printable version of this "Keep Homework Organized" checklist at http://www.newharbinger.com/41078. It's nice to have copies that you can mark on and then hang where you can refer to them easily.

Keeping Your Backpack Cleaned Out

For You to Know

Sometimes kids with ADHD stuff everything into their backpack and never organize it or clean it out. Then the backpack gets very heavy, and important papers can get lost, which is frustrating. When you organize your backpack and also clean it out every week, you will be able to find things more easily, and the backpack will be lighter to carry.

Joseph hated carrying his backpack. It was so heavy that his back hurt. Plus, he could never find anything in it. It seemed like his homework got lost as soon as he put it in there. One time his backpack started to smell, and he found a moldy apple in the bottom that he had forgotten was in there!

Joseph was amazed at all the stuff he found when he dumped everything out on the table. There was a note from his teacher that he was supposed to have given to his mom weeks before. His lost key to the house was buried at the bottom. The previous week's homework that he had worked so hard on was all crumpled up; he hadn't been able to find it when he went to turn it in.

First, Joseph put away or threw out all the things that didn't belong in his backpack. Then he put the things that did belong back in in such a way that he could find them. After that he drew a backpack map to remind himself where everything belonged. He found it so much easier to find what he needed. And he noticed his back no longer hurt.

For You to Do

You can find things in your backpack and keep it from getting too heavy if you organize it and keep it cleaned out. Ask an adult to help you, if you need it.

- Make a list of what belongs in your backpack. Examples include books for tonight's homework, homework folders, lunch bag, pencils, keys, note from or for the teacher, and gym clothes.

______________________	______________________
______________________	______________________
______________________	______________________
______________________	______________________

- Empty out your backpack. Then turn it upside down over a wastebasket and shake out any dirt and crumbs.
- Throw out or put away items that don't belong in your backpack.
- Sort everything into three piles: one for school supplies; one for papers, books, homework folders, and notebooks; and one for stuff to take back and forth to school, such as your lunch bag, mittens, keys, and school-to-home-to-school folder.
- Find a place in your backpack for each item that belongs.
- Put a reminder on your calendar to clean out your backpack once a week.

More to Do

An additional way to keep your backpack organized is to draw a map of it and label where everything goes. Then you can keep this map in a pocket of your backpack and another copy near where you keep the backpack at home. You can use your Backpack Map to put everything where it goes. (You can download a printable version of the blank "Backpack Map" at http://www.newharbinger.com/41078.)

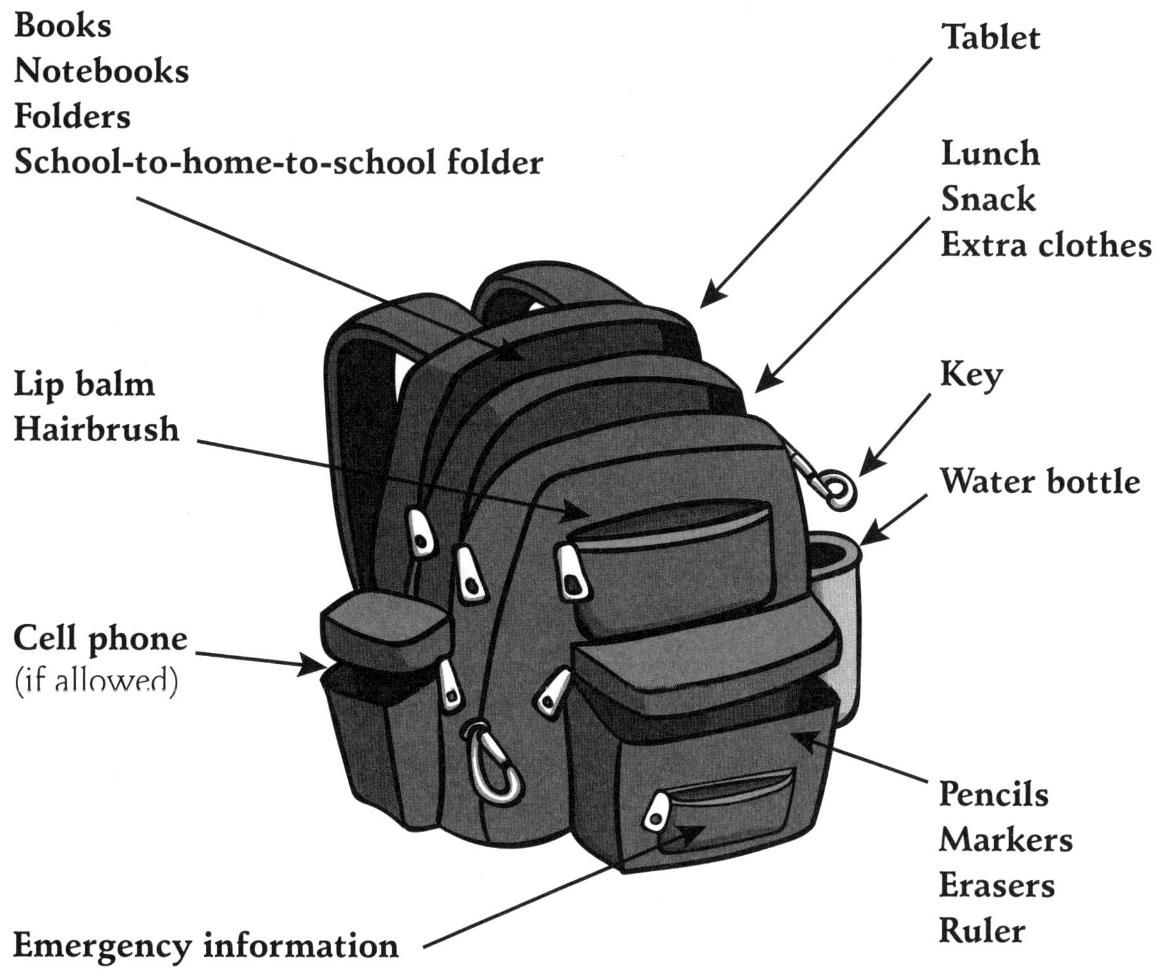

Sample Backpack Map

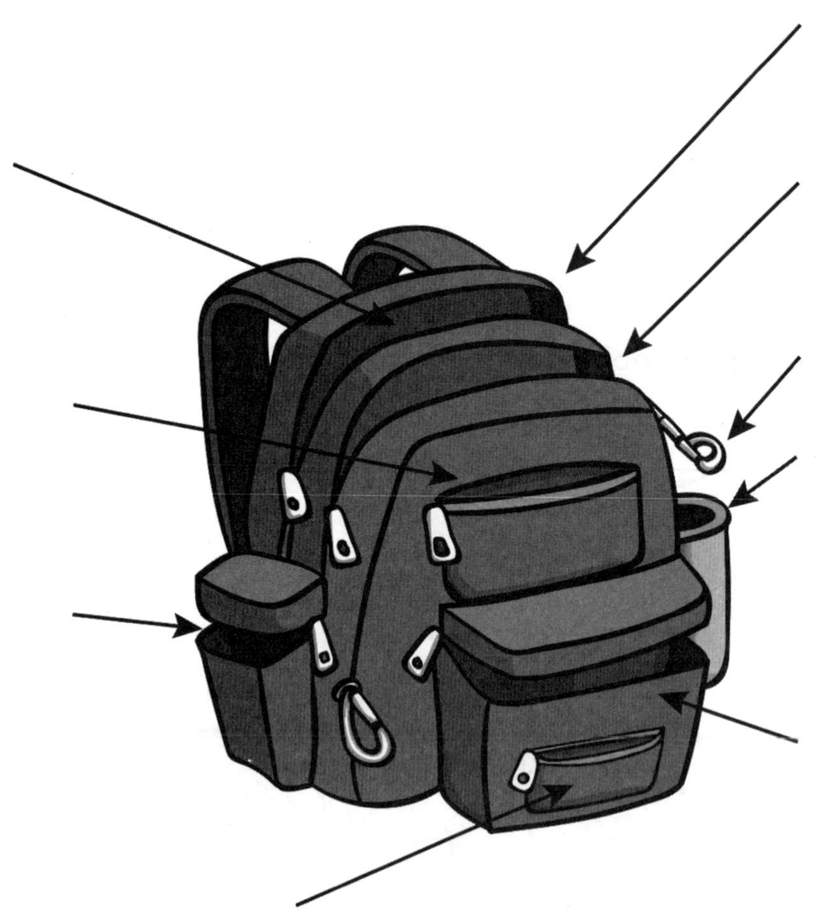

My Backpack Map

Staying Calm During a Test

For You to Know

Many kids with ADHD worry that they won't finish taking tests on time because they have trouble paying attention. Many find that their worry gets in the way of them doing well. You can plan ahead to avoid this kind of anxiety and practice a mindfulness skill that will help you stay calm and focused.

Natalie always felt worried when she had to take a test at school. She was afraid she wouldn't know the answers or finish in time. Sometimes her stomach hurt so badly during a test that she could hardly concentrate on the questions. This made it even harder to do well.

"Your worry about taking a test is called test anxiety," Natalie's therapist explained. "Let's plan ahead for the next test you have to take." The therapist helped Natalie put the important dates on her calendar so she knew when to start preparing for the test and when she would study. Then she set her intention to study for the test and to ask someone to explain the material and quiz her on it until she felt like she really knew what she needed to know.

She also listened to a meditation that guided her to practice staying calm while taking a test. The meditation helped her relax and focus during the actual test. She felt prepared and calm during the next test she took, finished on time, and earned a good grade!

For You to Do

Do you have test anxiety? Circle all the signs of test anxiety that you've experienced, and use the blank lines to add others.

I worry about how I'm going to do on a test.

I do other things when I should study.

My body feels some signs of anxiety before or during a test, such as:

- Headaches
- Sweating
- Fast heartbeat
- Dry mouth
- Shortness of breath
- Nausea
- Diarrhea
- Feeling too hot or cold

I have extra trouble concentrating because I worry about how I'm doing.

I keep changing my answers or get stuck.

I have unhelpful thoughts, such as *I will fail, so why try?*

I want to stay home from school when there is a test.

Other: ____

Other: ____

If you circled any of these, you probably have test anxiety. You can use the following skills to reduce it. Prevent and reduce anxiety by taking the following steps to prepare for a test:

1. Ask your parents to talk to your teachers about giving you extra time to take the test and providing a distraction-free place to take it. Most schools will do these things for students who have ADHD.
2. Put the test on your assignment calendar.
3. Plan ahead so you have plenty of time to study.
4. Mark your calendar for when you will study.
5. Build your confidence by studying and preparing for the test on several different days.
6. Ask a friend or family member to quiz you.
7. Give yourself a practice test, time yourself, and review anything you had trouble with.
8. Create a game plan for taking the test, such as answering the questions you know first and going back to the harder ones later.
9. Get enough sleep the night before the test.
10. Get some exercise before the test.

More to Do

To help yourself calm test anxiety, read or listen to the following calming meditation several times. Then remind yourself to do these steps while you take a test.

Close your eyes and imagine that you need to take a test.

Make sure you know when the test is.

Study until you know what you need to know.

Now imagine you are taking the test.

Notice when you feel anxious.

Tune in to how your body feels.

How does anxiety show up in your body?

However it shows up, accept it. Just let it be.

Breathe in through your nose to the count of four (1-2-3-4).

Breathe in calm and safety.

Breathe out through your mouth to the count of eight (1-2-3-4-5-6-7-8), as if you are blowing a huge bubble, and breathe out worry and stress.

Again, breathe in through your nose to the count of four (1-2-3-4).

Breathe in focus and calm.

Breathe out fear and worry to the count of eight (1-2-3-4-5-6-7-8).

Let go of your worry so you can focus on the test.

Say to yourself, "I am prepared. I can do this."

Imagine that you are doing well on the test.

Bring your attention back to the test.

Practice this meditation until you know it by heart.

When you feel anxious during a test, remind yourself to use these steps to calm your worry.

You can download an audio recording of this meditation, "Calm Your Test Anxiety," at http://www.newharbinger.com/41078.

Activity 33 Noticing What's Going on Around You

For You to Know

Kids with ADHD can sometimes have trouble paying attention to what's going on in their surroundings and in certain situations. If you practice noticing your surroundings and the situation you are in, you will be better able to stay calm and pay attention to the important things.

Logan had trouble paying attention. He often felt overwhelmed and easily distracted, and sometimes he forgot where he was and what he was supposed to be doing.

Logan and his therapist started playing a game called Say What You See, which helped him practice paying attention to what was going on around him. After trying this game a few times, Logan began playing it on his own wherever he was. When he did, he felt calmer and less distracted. Then he could pay attention to the most important things.

For You to Do

You can practice noticing what's around you by playing Say What You See. You can play it anywhere.

1. Without looking around, draw a picture of everything you can remember about where you are.

Before Looking

2. Now, take a deep breath in and blow it out slowly, as if you are blowing a huge bubble.

3. Look in front of you and say what you see. For example, if you are in your bedroom, you might say, "I see a closet, a brown dresser, a blue desk, and a window."

4. Now look to your left and say what you see. If you are in your classroom, you might say, "I can see a yellow wall; a big brown desk; my teacher, who is a lady with brown hair grading a paper; a girl sitting at the desk next to mine; and a poster with flowers on the wall."
5. Now look to your right and say what you see. If you are outside, maybe you'd say, "I see a big tree with green leaves, a white house, a red car, a dog, and the road. I see traffic speeding by."
6. Now look up and say what you see. If you are in a store, you might say, "I see lights on the white ceiling. I see heat vents and some silver pipes."
7. Now look down and say what you see. You might say, "I see a brown carpet with yellow flowers on it."
8. Is there anything you need to pay attention to? If you are outside, maybe you need to pay attention to the cars so they don't hit you. If you are in class, maybe you need to pay attention to the teacher or schoolwork. If you are in a store, maybe you need to pay attention to what you are buying or to other people, making sure you are not in their way.

9. Now draw a picture of everything you can remember about where you are.

After Looking

Look at the two pictures you drew and see what you forgot in the first picture and remembered in the second picture.

Are there things you forgot to put in your first picture that you remembered to draw in your second picture? If so, circle them.

After you have played this game a few times, you can practice looking at your surroundings wherever you are to help yourself stay calm and safe, and to pay attention to the important things.

Now draw a picture of the most important thing to pay attention to where you are right now.

The Most Important Thing

Getting Along with Others

For You to Know

Some kids with ADHD are very good at making friends, but many haven't yet mastered some of the social skills they need to make friends and get along with others. You can practice these skills and be mindful about using them to create friendships more easily.

Grace wished she had more friends. She felt like no one liked her. She often felt rejected when other kids didn't ask her to play or include her in their activities. She wondered what she might be doing that was keeping her from having friends.

With her therapist's help, Grace started noticing some things she did that other kids probably didn't like. She became aware that her being hyperactive and talking all the time was annoying her classmates. Then she practiced skills to help her make friends. She learned to be mindful of paying attention to the person she was talking to. She practiced looking at the person, saying hi, waiting her turn to speak, listening to others instead of talking nonstop, sharing, being kind, showing interest in the other person, and respecting other people's things.

At first it was hard to pay attention to her own behavior and to learn new skills. But it got easier with practice. And she was thrilled when she made a new friend and had someone to sit with at lunch.

For You to Do

Circle the things that you do that might make it harder to make friends.

Nonstop talking

Being distracted

Being bossy

Not listening

Interrupting

Changing the topic

Breaking rules

Being hyper

Being loud

Not showing interest in the other person

Talking about yourself too much

Being angry

Not sharing

Breaking other people's things

Now place a red *X* next to things on the list above you will do less of.

On the list below, circle the things that you do or could do that might make it easier to make friends.

Making eye contact

Listening

Showing interest in the other person

Waiting until the other person finishes speaking

Asking what the other person wants to do

Talking about what the other person is talking about

Talking quietly

Quieting your body

Staying calm

Following the rules

Sharing

Being careful with the other person's things

Now place a happy face ☺ next to the things you will do more often.

Pick one behavior that you put a red *X* next to and write down what you can change about that behavior that will work better for your friendships. Ask for help with this, if you need it.

Behavior: ____

What I can change about this behavior: ______________________________

____

Practice changing this behavior for one week.

More to Do

Practicing Mindful Social Skills for Making Friends will help you make friends. Practice with someone you know well, such as a family member. Then when you feel comfortable doing the skills, try using them with people you might like to be friends with.

- *Making eye contact:* Without staring, look at another person closely enough to see what color his or her eyes are. Say to yourself, *I see your eyes are (insert color).*
- *Offering a mindful greeting:* To greet someone, look at the person and say, "Hi, my name is (your name). What's your name?" Then, when the person says, "Hi, my name is (the other person's name), it's nice to meet you," you can say, "It's nice to meet you, too."
- *Waiting for your turn:* When you are waiting to do something, such as answer a question in class, or to get something, such as lunch, notice who might already be waiting to do the same thing. Wait until it is your turn.
- *Sharing:* Let someone use or have something of yours, such as a swing, a toy, or your dessert. Take turns so you both get to use it. Share something three times this week.
- *Showing interest:* Show others that you are interested in getting to know them. You can ask them questions about themselves: What's your name? What grade are you in? Who is your teacher? Do you like math? What did you do for fun this weekend? Have you watched any good movies lately? Ask at least one person questions about himself or herself this week.
- *Respecting other people's things:* When you are using or playing with something that belongs to someone else, make sure it's okay for you to use it. Be careful, and use it gently; keep it clean, and put it away when you are done. This week be respectful of something that belongs to someone else.

- *Being kind:* How can you be kind to someone? You might say something nice, such as "I like your T-shirt. It's really pretty." You could let someone go ahead of you in line. If you notice that a classmate forgot a snack, you could offer him or her some of yours. Be kind three times this week.

- *Being helpful:* What can you do that might be helpful? Perhaps you could open the door for someone, pick up something a person dropped, help an individual carry something, help someone learn something, let another person use your pencil, or set the table. Practice being helpful three times this week.

- *Listening:* Listen to what someone is saying, and let the person finish before you say anything. Look at the person while you listen to show you are interested. Then say something that is about what the person is talking about. For example, if Sally is talking about going to the trampoline park, let her finish talking before asking her something about what it was like, such as "What park did you go to? Which trampoline did you like the best? Have you ever been there before?" Listen carefully to someone this week.

You can practice these social skills by *role-playing.* Ask an adult to help you pretend you are using your social skills. The adult can take the role of someone your age you would like to be friends with. You take on the role of you. Practice making eye contact, greeting the person, listening, asking questions about what the other person is saying, waiting your turn, sharing, and being kind and helpful. Now ask the adult to pretend to be you, and you pretend to be someone you want to be friends with. The adult can practice the skills while you act out how the person you want to be friends with might respond. Be sure to notice what you learn from being in this role.

What skills did you practice this week? Include who you did them with, what happened, and how you felt.

Skills: ____

Who did you do them with? ______________________________

____

What happened? ______________________________________

____

How did you feel? _____________________________________

____

What can you do differently next time? ___________________

____

Acknowledgments

My deepest thanks to my clients and my daughter for teaching me that although ADHD can make many things more challenging, it can also offer tremendous benefits of creativity, brilliance, energy, and joy.

My heartfelt thanks to Wendy Millstine, from New Harbinger Publications, who invited me to write this workbook and who guided, supported, and encouraged me along the way. Many thanks to all those at New Harbinger who read, reread, edited, and helped me create and shape this workbook.

Debra Burdick, LCSW, also known as "The Brain Lady," is an international expert on mindfulness and attention deficit/hyperactivity disorder (ADHD). She is author of *ADHD Non-Medication Treatment and Skills for Children and Teens; Mindfulness Skills for Kids and Teens; Mindfulness for Teens with ADHD; Mindfulness Skills Workbook for Clinicians and Clients;* the *Mindfulness Skills for Kids* card deck and games; and several mindfulness CDs/MP3s. She teaches all-day workshops, including *100 Brain-Changing Mindfulness Strategies for Clinical Practice, Childhood ADHD,* and *Mindfulness Toolkit for Kids and Teens.*

A licensed clinical social worker and board-certified neurotherapist, Burdick recently retired from private practice to focus on writing, speaking, and her grandchildren. She incorporates mindfulness skills in all areas of her life and work, and has extensive experience helping children and adults with ADHD, including her own daughter. Burdick's work has been featured on radio (Attention Talk Radio, ADHD Support Talk Radio, and Doctors of the USA), in print media (*The Wall Street Journal*, Connecticut newspaper *The Day*, and *Self Improvement*), and on television (*Parenting Powers* and *Restoring Health Holistically*). Visit www.thebrainlady.com for more information.

Foreword writer **Edward M. Hallowell, MD**, is a child and adult psychiatrist, leading authority in the field of ADHD, *New York Times* bestselling author, and world-renowned speaker. He is host of *Distraction*—a weekly podcast series, and founder of The Hallowell Centers for Cognitive and Emotional Health in Boston MetroWest; New York, NY; San Francisco, CA; and Seattle, WA. Learn more at www.drhallowell.com.

MORE BOOKS *from* NEW HARBINGER PUBLICATIONS

MASTER OF MINDFULNESS

How to Be Your Own Superhero in Times of Stress

978-1626254640 / US $14.95

LITTLE FLOWER YOGA FOR KIDS

A Yoga & Mindfulness Program to Help Your Child Improve Attention & Emotional Balance

978-1608827923 / US $19.95

DON T LET YOUR EMOTIONS RUN YOUR LIFE FOR KIDS

A DBT-Based Skills Workbook to Help Children Manage Mood Swings, Control Angry Outbursts & Get Along with Others

978-1626258594 / US $16.95

MINDFUL DISCIPLINE

A Loving Approach to Setting Limits & Raising an Emotionally Intelligent Child

978-1608828845 / US $17.95

ANXIETY RELIEF FOR KIDS

On-the-Spot Strategies to Help Your Child Overcome Worry, Panic & Avoidance

978-1626259539 / US $16.95

BALANCED & BAREFOOT

How Unrestricted Outdoor Play Makes for Strong, Confident & Capable Children

978-1626253735 / US $16.95

new**harbinger**publications

1-800-748-6273 / newharbinger.com

(VISA, MC, AMEX / prices subject to change without notice)

Follow Us

Don't miss out on new books in the subjects that interest you.
Sign up for our **Book Alerts** at **newharbinger.com/bookalerts**

new harbinger
CELEBRATING
40 YEARS